VERMONT WOMEN, NATIVE AMERICANS & AFRICAN AMERICANS

VERMONT WOMEN, NATIVE AMERICANS & AFRICAN AMERICANS

Out of the Shadows of History

CYNTHIA D. BITTINGER

Charleston · London

THE
History
PRESS

Published by The History Press
Charleston, SC 29403
www.historypress.net

Copyright © 2012 by Cynthia D. Bittinger
All rights reserved

Front cover, left to right: Emma Willard, educator, Middlebury. *Courtesy of the Middlebury College Archives*; George Washington Henderson, 1877 University of Vermont graduate. *Courtesy of Special Collections, Bailey/Howe Library at the University of Vermont*; Marion Annette Anderson, first female African American graduate of Middlebury College. *Courtesy of Northfield–Mount Herman Archives.*

Back cover: Drawing of Molly Ockett by Danna B. Nickerson. *Courtesy of Bethel Historical Society, Bethel, Maine*; teacher Edna Beard of Orange, 1906. *Courtesy of the Vermont Historical Society, Barre, Vermont.*

First published 2012

Manufactured in the United States

ISBN 978.1.60949.262.5

Library of Congress CIP data applied for.

To my students, may they appreciate the past

To teachers, may they gain the respect they are due

Contents

Acknowledgements

What part of the past will be carried into the future? That is the motivation behind this book. If we look at history and try to see the views of Vermont Native Americans, African Americans and women, what do we see? I see many new stories that have not been told. Many researchers, journalists, filmmakers and historians agree. I have added their names and publications to the list of sources at the end of the book. I have read over their materials many times and distilled them into this one, hopefully accessible, source. Their research and writing provided steps to create a past that needs to be carried over into the future. Readers of this book are encouraged to read books and websites noted in the sources for a more in-depth treatment of these subjects.

I would like to thank the Community College of Vermont, the Wilder office, the online team, the library and Linda Gabrielson, academic dean, for giving me the opportunity to teach Vermont history since 1994 and for supporting this book project. By teaching the essential objectives in a survey course, I realized that a fuller narrative including African Americans, Native Americans and women could be a contribution to the teaching at that institution.

I wish to praise the Vermont Women's History Project, a website run by the Vermont Historical Society, for providing important biographies of women. The volunteers and interns who have written materials for this website provide an important educational resource.

ACKNOWLEDGEMENTS

I wish to thank Vermont Public Radio and editor Betty Smith for encouraging me as a commentator for over ten years. The series about the history of women in Vermont, featured each March for women's history month, is an important part of my research.

Both Road Scholar (formerly Elderhostel) and OSHER Lifelong Learning Institute, an affiliate of the University of Vermont, have sponsored my presentations and encouraged my research.

The Vermont Historical Society and the Calvin Coolidge Memorial Foundation have also sponsored my presentations and research. I thank both organizations for the emphasis on teaching teachers this new information, for teachers and their students will carry forth a new narrative of inclusion. Melody Walker, a member of the Elu band of Abenakis; Lynn Bonfield, a Peacham Historical Society expert; and Jane Williamson, director of Rokeby, all read drafts and added important material and criticism. The staff at the Howe Library of Hanover, New Hampshire, ordered book after book across the state for my research.

Digital images were a challenge to obtain at the proper resolution for publication. Each image is credited so that readers can find those sources. Most helpful were Nancy Osgood, Nancy Hoggson, Alan Berolzheimer, John Moody and Judy F. Brown of the Norwich Historical Society; Paul Carnahan and Judy Barwood of the Vermont Historical Society; Susan MacIntire of the Shoreham Historical Society; Maureen Fisher Fletcher of the Grafton Historical Society; Diane McInerney of the Division for Historic Preservation; Chief Don Stevens, Nulhegan band of the Coosuk, Abenaki nation; Brad Seymour of the New York State Museum; Ina Smith of the Poultney Historical Society; Sylvia Bugbee, Prudence Doherty and Sharon Thayer of the University of Vermont Archives; Rachel Muse of the Vermont State Archives and Records Administration; Renee Fox of the Canterbury Shaker Village; Vera Longtoe Sheehan of the Elnu Abenaki tribe; Joyce Mandeville and Bill Pelton of the T.W. Wood Gallery; artist Louise Minks; Judy Antle of the Missisquoi Historical Society; Henry Duffy of Saint Gaudens National Historic Site; Jackie Penny of the American Antiquarian Society; Jim Davidson of the Rutland Historical Society; Nancy Young of the Sophia Smith Collection, Smith College; Danielle M. Rougeau of the Middlebury College Archives; Jennifer Donaldson of the Woodstock History Center; Kate Bradley of the Coolidge Foundation; Jack Herlihy of Lowell National Historical Park; Liz Nelson of the Old Stone House Museum; Peter Weis of the Northfield, Mount Herman School Archives; Paul G. Zeller of the Williamstown Historical Society; Andy

Kolovos, archivist and folklorist at the Vermont Folklife Center; and Julie Bartlett Nelson of the Calvin Coolidge Presidential Library and Museum, Forbes Library, Northampton, Massachusetts. A special thanks goes to Brian Lindner of National Life, who provided prints for the book.

My husband, Bill, listened and encouraged. His support was essential to completing the book. A thank-you goes to The History Press and Whitney Tarella for encouraging this project from beginning to end.

INTRODUCTION

In 2012, Vermont Public Radio featured a Vermont edition during which commentators and the public were grappling with the question "Who is a Vermonter?" In the past, that could quickly be answered with the reply of "a Yankee," meaning a white person who was born in and grew up in the state. They were often called Yankees since they would have descended from British settlers. Dorothy Canfield Fisher, writing in the 1950s, had relatives who could remember the War of 1812, and she wrote *Vermont Tradition* to see "how Vermont history shaped, molded and created Vermont character."[1] Her book featured political and military heroes Ethan Allen and Justin Morrill and even a poet, Robert Frost. However, with today's world, where 49 percent of Vermonters are "transplants," a new narrative should unfold. Looking back at history—at people of color, the original native inhabitants and the role of women—brings a new view of who was here all along but overlooked.

Native American history, African American history and women's history (or women's studies) often depict their subjects as "oppressed and passive victims."[2] Of course, racism and sexism did exist in Vermont, as it did in the rest of United States of America, and the natives, blacks and women were the targets of discrimination. Yet Vermont was founded with a constitution that was the most enlightened document of its time in 1777. It declared that slavery was banned and men did not need property to vote. So Vermont, as a republic, had a strong sense of self and exceptionalism.

The settlers pouring into Vermont from southern New England after 1763 at the end of the French and Indian War brought with them their attitudes of enlightenment. They also were imbued with a frontier mentality that would be trouble for Native Americans but would encourage the settlers to be persistent. They were readers who would include women and children in the literate world. The Vermont Constitution mandated a school for every town. After all, in farm life, all hands in the house were to be put to work. However, there was something more in this new republic. Somehow the door was opened for change. Minorities and women willing to reach higher could sometimes gain credit. Often the rationale was religion—that one should change to be closer to God or to follow the equality read about in the Bible. Sometimes it was judging a person by the quality of his or her character, not the color of her skin or her role only as a mother.

I have tried in this small volume to present positive people and positive experiences and to use their own words in many cases. Looking at letters, diaries and firsthand accounts helps uncover what the people really did think in their time. They were not perfect. They often exhibited the mindset of their times. However, I have chosen to highlight those who wanted to better their race, their gender or their sense of place. Those who wanted to leave a fairer, more caring world made the list. However, I did not want to just place people in categories and give short sketches. I wanted to present a fuller picture of their times and their contributions. Most of those described have not been part of the history books of the past. With a focus on landscape, military battles and government, natives, blacks and women are usually not included unless they participated in a battle or ran for office. Of course, official recognition and acceptance is the goal of a more just society. Therefore, those who did break the glass ceilings and did gain recognition in the state government or in the national arena are highlighted.

As we move forward, these past injustices are largely forgotten. But that is not why we study history. Women and people of color "have been denied a usable history."[3] There is a need to know how one fits into the American and Vermont story. Without this history, one can have "a distorted sense of self and a sense of inferiority based on a denigration or elimination of their group experiences."[4] More importantly, the history of women and their public activities outside the home show that "women's vision is an integral part of our nation's distinctive democratic political culture."[5] I am offering this history to change the narrative of Vermont's past, present and future.

Part I
Natives On the Land

We Are Here

"An Abenaki Poem"

As we stand tall, we hold each other's hand.
We want you to understand who and what we are.
In our body, and soul, we are Abenaki Indians.
As we yell, "we do exist."
Look at us! We are real, inside and out.
Put us on your list. We have been brave.
We cannot look the other way.
We are here to stay. You hear our drums play.
We bring peace from our chief who stands proud on our ground that we share.
We all breathe the same air. We drink the same water.
Our ancestors are still here. If you quit, you can hear them cry.
They still want to know why; Can't you accept us?
Open your eyes. We are here and, stand proud.
We are Abenaki.[6]

Sylvanus Johnson, age eleven, was a white captive taken by the Abenakis in 1754 from Charlestown, New Hampshire. It only took about six months for the captive child to become part of the Abenaki society. He was accepted as a warrior in a tribe based in St. Francis, Canada, where the boy could "brandish a tomahawk or bend the bow."[7] He spent four years with the Indians and one with some French settlers, thus becoming fluent in the Indian tongue and conversant in French; he forgot the English language. He wore Indian clothing and moccasins, ate their diet and learned their pace of travel and "techniques of wilderness survival."[8] When Major Rogers and his men destroyed the village of St. Francis in 1759, they returned with Sabatis, an Indian they captured, and he and Sylvanus were brothers, so to speak, having lived and fought together. (Sabatis was the son of a white captive and his Indian wife.)

Sylvanus considered the English settlers, rather than the Indians, to be the enemy. He probably wanted to stay with the Indians. After all, he learned to worship with the French and had become a Catholic, a religion abhorrent to the English settlers, who were followers of the Protestant Congregational Church. If Sylvanus had written a memoir, the story would have helped bridge a cultural gap. More understanding between the British and Abenakis could have developed. Sylvanus might have helped us find the hidden history of the Abenakis, the first peoples in Vermont. He could have translated their language and written down their history. Without written history, it is so difficult to reconstruct the past. He could have presented the actual "multifaceted phenomenon" of the English and Abenaki Indian-white frontier in Vermont.[9] Instead, his mother, Susanna, penned a religious polemic after being urged on by her minister that justified the treatment of natives in Vermont and New Hampshire. Despite the kindnesses shown to her by the St. Francis Indians, she had seen too many deaths and too much starvation to want anything but peace and to not see or hear another Indian. She wrote in her summary at the end of her memoir:

> *The savages are driven beyond the lakes, and our country has no enemies. The gloomy wilderness that 50 years ago secreted the Indian and beast of prey, has vanished away; and the thrifty farm smiles in its stead: the Sundays that were then employed in guarding a fort, are now quietly devoted to worship: the tomahawk and scalping knife have given place to the plough-share and sickle, and prosperous husbandry now thrives, where the terrors of death once chilled us with fear.*[10]

Finding Early Evidence of Indians in Vermont

Yet Susanna was wrong. The Abenakis did live in Vermont, but not often in plain sight. There were "enclaves of western Abenakis" in Vermont preserving their cultural and political identity.[11] Luckily, there have been a few historians, ethnologists and archaeologists who have sifted through what they could find as evidence to declare that Indians had a presence in Vermont from after the ice age to the present day. Early archaeological evidence has been discovered and documented.

Even though the area we call Vermont was one of the last places to be inhabited by humans, archaeologists have found evidence dating from over 11,300 years ago.[12] The Paleoindians had traveled over a land bridge from Asia to Alaska and then went from west to east and from south to north in North America. The fluted points used in those times for hunting woolly mammoths and mastodons have been found in Brandon, Orwell, St. Albans, Swanton and East Highgate (the Reagan site). These weapons have also been uncovered along Otter Creek and the Winooski and Connecticut Rivers. The marine resources of the Champlain Sea would have been available until about 7400 BC, so fish and other sea animals were part of an Indian diet. During the Archaic period, about 6000 BC, big-game hunting ended as the wooly mammoths became extinct, but small game was plentiful. Some natives migrated from the northern area above Vermont, now Canada, to Vermont, as did some from southern New England. Archaeologists in Vergennes have found evidence such as chipped stone artifacts used to treat meat and make hides into clothes. Dugout canoes and containers were created by the natives from hides and tree bark in this early period.

There are forty-nine archaeological sites in the town of Shelburne.

Sites within the historic boundaries of Shelburne Farms include ones located on Shelburne Point to the north; the shores of McCabes Brook and the LaPlatte River to the east; the wetlands near Saxton's Point to the west; and an area in the center of the estate, near a small stream leading to the LaPlatte River. Although further study is required, one archaeologist has speculated that projectile points and other artifacts found at the latter site could indicate either a "very large settlement—one of the largest recorded anywhere in Vermont from this time period—or the site of recurring occupations over an extended period of time."[13]

A 2012 movie by local filmmakers produced by Nora Jacobson concerns stories from the state of Vermont and begins with a long section on Native Americans. That should not be surprising since most of us who have taken American history know that native peoples were in North America before the European explorers and settlers ever landed on the continent. Yet that introductory material would be surprising to the historians writing Vermont history from the eighteenth century to 1968. They often began their books with a discussion of explorers such as Samuel de Champlain, the first white man to see the territory of Vermont. Of course he interacted with Indians, but they wrote summaries such as this one: "Vermont was a no man's land, a passageway for French and Indian raiding parties seeking to harass the English settlements to the south and east."[14] Fort Dummer, near Brattleboro, was established by British settlers in 1724 and represented the first permanent settlement by whites in Vermont. The French predated this settlement with a fort on Isle La Motte in 1666 and with Chimney Point in 1690, but these did not last.

Historians writing books and articles right up to the 1960s began their books by describing Vermont's first settlers—here meaning the British going north from Massachusetts and Connecticut. Why had these scholars missed the earlier story of Native American settlement? Was it ethnocentrism? Lack of sources? Lack of imagination? It certainly was history hidden from them and thus not shared with the citizens of Vermont and the rest of America. It was a disservice to us all. The winners usually do write history. The French had allied with the Abenakis, the tribal group in Vermont, and then lost the French and Indian War to the British. In 1763, Britain won that battle for North America, and they wrote the victorious story. Then when the Americans revolted against the British Crown, they in turn wrote the story as winners. The Abenakis had, for the most part, sided with the French, and then, after the French and Indian War, with the British, and they lost their chance to write history or keep their claim to the land in Vermont when the rebels won.

In 1996, Rosalind P. Hanson of the New Hampshire Antiquarian Society suggested that historians look deeper into the native history of New England. She characterized early town historians as writing about "vicious acts of the uncivilized red man" on the one hand, and poets, novelists and biographers on the other "extolling the noble savages who once roamed our countryside but are no longer here."[15] Hanson continued to conduct research because there was interest in the Indian culture and because Indians had helped the European immigrants survive. Yet the Indians were "cruelly and wrongly evicted over and over again from their homelands and deprived of their

Fort Dummer, the first British settlement, was built in 1724 in what is now Brattleboro. The fort was to protect southern New England from Indian attacks. *Courtesy of the National Life Insurance Company.*

right to live as free men, women, and children in our Land of Liberty and Justice."[16] In Charles C. Mann's book, *1491: New Revelations of the Americas Before Columbus,* he wrote that in the 1970s there was finally interest in "peering through the colonial records to the Indian lives beneath."[17]

Abenaki means "those living at sunrise" or "at the dawnland."[18] As the dawn rose on the East Coast of North America, the natives there saw it before anyone else. On a map of Wabanaki Country, or the Dawnland region, the Algonquian-speaking people are Abenakis, Passamaquoddy-Maliseets and Micmacs.[19] The Western Abenakis are based in Vermont.[20] "New England's major river valleys…held large, permanent villages, many nestled in constellations of suburban hamlets and hunting camps" with summer and winter locations.[21] Historian Jan Albers observed that the native people lived on "favored lands in Vermont: on bluffs over the Otter Creek, Missisquoi, Lamoille, and Winooski Rivers, from the Northeast Kingdom to the Taconics, from the shores of Lake Champlain to the tops of the Green Mountains."[22] As Albers surveyed the land of Vermont before "white expansion," she re-created this setting:

> [T]*he trees grew thick in the land that would become Vermont. There were a few clearings along the shores of lakes and rivers, where native people had practiced agriculture. Some of these meadows were filling up with brush, for the women who had cleared them had fled to the mountains or were dead of the smallpox. The roads were water roads, bubbling quietly beneath the arching trees. On land, ancient paths ran from the water to the mountains, to territories marked with symbols of their human stewards. The salmon ran strong and the mammals scurried at the edge of the woods. It was a quiet world, of snapping twigs and trilling birds and the soft thudding of suede-covered feet on dirt trails. No one then alive could anticipate how quickly such a world could be lost.*[23]

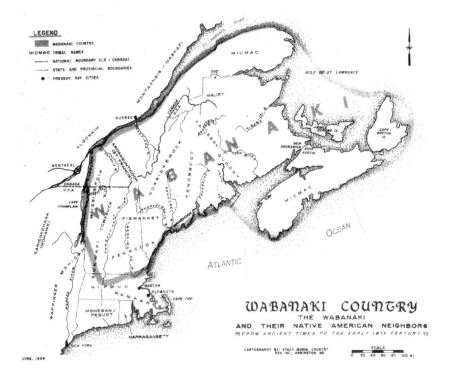

Abenaki tribal communities were part of the Algonquin brotherhood and the Wabanaki Confederacy. This map shows Lake Champlain dividing Mohawks to the west from Abenakis to the east. *Courtesy of Chief Don Stevens, Nulhegan band of the Coosuk-Abenaki nation.*

Who retrieved this early, prewritten history that we now study in the new, post-1960 Vermont history books? Fish and game warden Tom Daniels was one person who studied Vermont for more than forty years and wrote about *Vermont Indians* as early as 1963.[24] He was born in Orwell and claimed both Chippewa and Sioux heritage. Daniels found seventy campsites, three caves and two rock shelters with Indian artifacts in his Vermont explorations. His booklet was self-published and probably did not receive wide distribution. Since he was a game warden, academics must have dismissed much of his work even though he was important in finding sites and increasing awareness of the Native American culture and evidence in Vermont.

Historians credit Gordon M. Day, who searched for New England's native past and found it. He devoted most of his life to providing the evidence and opening the door to this new interpretation of state history. Gordon Day began his life in 1911 in Albany, Vermont, a town in Orleans County in the Northeast Kingdom. As a child, he played with children who were part Abenaki and knew the area as a place for natives to hunt and trap. In his adult years, he initially set out to study forest ecology, but after serving in World War II, he decided to "devote himself entirely to saving Abenaki culture from oblivion."[25] He became an ethnologist, someone who compares and analyzes the origins, distribution, technology, religion, language and social structure of the ethnic, racial and/or national divisions of humanity.

Day based his initial observations on the fact that "aboriginal subsistence activities and village life had fundamentally affected large sections of eastern woodlands" before European contact.[26] He wrote that historians did not know this history because they had an "ethnocentric, arm's length picture of Indians" and relied on accounts from "enemies, victims, captives and conquerors."[27] Day turned to French records and Indian traditions. He found that "until the end of the 18th century, the village of Missisquoi, located near present-day Swanton, Vermont, served as a political hub for Western Abenaki scattered through the Champlain Valley. By the end of the 1920s the site had been abandoned, although Abenakis continued to live in enclaves in the surrounding area and throughout the state."[28] They even collected rent for land there until 1800. Thus Day is credited with documenting the history of the Abenakis in Vermont for American historians.

First Contact Between Cultures

When the first Europeans met the natives, they found "strikingly healthy specimens. Eating an incredibly nutritious diet, working hard but not broken by toil, the [native] people of New England were taller and more robust than those who wanted to move in."[29] Indians observed the Europeans as dirty; they did not take baths regularly, and they were "physically weak, sexually untrustworthy, atrociously ugly, and just plain smelly," using dirty handkerchiefs.[30] Yet these handsome Indians had no immunity in the face of European diseases that the explorers brought with them, and in 1616 and 1617, natives died by the thousands.[31] In 1633 and 1639, smallpox decimated even more natives, leaving them with just 10 percent of their prior population.[32]

The natives who did survive lived with a "light touch" on the land since they believed that objects were "animate in some way."[33] They believed that there was no creator for the earth since it always existed. There was no need for personal ownership, only stewardship. "Gluskabe" made all things, with the most important being animals to hunt and plants to help man live.

Of course, the first British settlements were in Massachusetts, where natives helped them adjust to their new environment. The Indian named Squanto showed them how to plant corn and told them where to fish. He had been captured by explorers and taken to Spain and England, so upon his return to America, he could communicate with the new settlers, but he could not keep them from wanting to set up villages and farms and thus pushing the frontier of settlement farther north. At that time, the Appalachian Mountains were a barrier to western development.

Clearly, the reason why early white settlers could take land when they surveyed it was because there was so much available that natives did not need. The epidemics and plagues of 1616, 1617, 1675 and the 1690s had destroyed a large portion of the native population, probably 90 percent.[34]

French Dominance in North America

The French seemed to have a perfect plan to conquer the riches of the New World. As historian Jan Albers wrote, "For the French, the great attraction was extraction, particularly of the hides of fur-bearing mammals; communities might come later."[35] She continued, "From the early 17th century, the French were establishing trading outposts geared to serving the European rage for hats made of beaver pelts."[36] The French also had soft power: religion. This new force would change the way natives looked at the world. Traditional Indian cures had not stopped the scourges of European diseases, but the European medicines proffered by Jesuit priests proved effective since Frenchmen lived through these illnesses.

The French learned the Abenaki language and offered protection against the Iroquois of New York, allies of the British.[37] Frenchmen justified that they were in the New World with "the Indians' consent."[38] After all, the first European fort was the French-built Sainte Anne on Isle La Motte, an island in Lake Champlain. The French even offered the natives muskets for defense. The Abenakis also traded with the British when that was profitable, and these new trading networks did alter the Abenakis' ability to fend for themselves.[39] They now became dependent on new material goods such as

Abenakis on snowshoes come to trade beaver pelts with the French for guns. The drawings are the work of Roy F. Heinrich and Herbert Morton Stoops. *Courtesy of the National Life Insurance Company.*

iron, brass, glass and mirrors. They would also need guns and gunpowder for the many battles ahead.

In the 1740s, the Western Abenakis, with their French alliance, could keep the British settlers out of Vermont. In 1754, "two good-sized communities of Indians and some French settlers" lived near the Missisquoi River.[40] The French operated a sawmill on land in Swanton leased from the Abenakis. Some Abenakis were scouts for the French in the French and Indian War against the British. "Missisquoi, St. Francis, and Becancour were crucial sources of manpower for the French war effort."[41] The French actually wanted the Abenakis to settle down, till the soil and become Christians. They even imported workers from France to build them a village in Canada for that purpose, Sillary in 1638. In 1731, the French fortified Chimney Point and built a fort on Crown Point, the New York side of Lake Champlain. They decided to grant seigneuries on both sides of the lake—a seigneur would own the land and have farmers tend it. By the 1740s, about one thousand Frenchmen lived in the Champlain Valley, but the settlement model did not seem to take hold. Extraction of furs was more important to the French.

Montcalm Trying to Stop the Massacre. In 1757, 1,800 Indian warriors captured Fort William Henry in New York, and the French could not stop them from taking revenge on the British. *Courtesy of the Library of Congress.*

The British planned outposts and trained rangers to fight Indians. The Western Abenakis would hear from refugees from southern New England that the British had pushed them out by 1676. From 1723 to 1727, Grey Lock and his Indian supporters fought the British settlers from his hideout in Vermont. He was actually a Woronoke Indian from Massachusetts, but he based himself in the northern end of Lake Champlain.[42] He raided towns along the Connecticut River and Northampton, Massachusetts, but did not stir up the Iroquois in New York. Fear of Grey Lock brought about the building by the British of Fort Dummer, a blockhouse near Brattleboro. From there, the British sought to destroy Indian villages with their crops in nearby fields. Benning Wentworth, governor of New Hampshire, reported that 10 percent of his settlers were on guard duty, but fear was a constant, with killings and taking of captives almost weekly. Grey Lock never made peace with the Yankees, but they honored him by naming the highest peak in the Berkshires for him.

In 1757, about 245 Abenakis from Vermont villages, plus members of the Penobscot nation, were part of the 1,800 Indian warriors at the capture of Fort William Henry at the southern end of Lake George in New York. That victory in warfare showed the natives at their most violent, killing and scalping those who had already surrendered to the French. The Abenakis also fought their own war without the French against the British, with attacks and taking captives such as Susanna Johnson and her family.

Captives: Eyewitnesses to Abenaki History

Reading eyewitness accounts is one way to piece together the early history of interaction between settlers and natives. Whose biography did the early settlers read? Susanna Johnson's. She was a survivor of capture from the Fort Number 4 area near Charlestown, New Hampshire. Her eyewitness account is important since she was part of the evolving relationship between Euro-Americans and Native Americans. (Abenakis often called whites Euro-Americans.) She had been brought up to be a proper British settler, worshiping in the Protestant Church and trying to be obedient to her husband and church. At the beginning of her memoir, she described Charlestown as a place where "the Indians were numerous, and associated in a friendly way with the whites."[43] So she might have had an open mind. Her own husband had a store where he exchanged items with Indians in trade for furs.

Yet she was fearful for her safety and that of her family. After all, she could not see any organized government to back them up. The captain in charge of the fort was Captain Stevens, and he had been a prisoner at St. Francis in Canada, so he knew what it was like to be under Indian rule and would be alert to their security needs. Yet Susanna rapidly became aware of the danger lurking in the dark. She wrote, "The gloominess of the rude forest, the distance from friends and competent defense, and the daily inroads and nocturnal yells of hostile Indians, awaken those keen apprehensions and anxieties which conception can only picture."[44]

Just when she and her husband decided to pack up and leave for peaceful Northfield, Massachusetts, the Indians struck at her home. On August 30, 1754, eleven Indians awakened her family and neighbors who were staying there. Susanna was about to give birth, so the timing could not have been more unfortunate. She gave birth the next day in a town we now call Cavendish, Vermont. She was still forced to continue on their path to Canada but was given a horse for travel until starvation forced the group to kill it for food. Susanna put her faith in "that Being who has the power to

Mrs. Susanna Johnson was captured by Indians and gave birth to a baby girl on August 31, 1754. Mrs. Johnson's memoir recounts her life with the French and the Native Americans. *Courtesy of the National Life Insurance Company.*

save."[45] Her religion obviously colored her point of view. She did arrive at Odanak, the St. Francis Abenaki village, which was on the St. Francis River, about ninety miles north of Lake Memphremagog.

Her narrative stated that after forty-five days of living at St. Francis, she felt qualified to describe it. She wrote that the village "contained about thirty wigwams which were thrown disorderly into a clump. There was a church, in which mass was held every night and morning, and every Sunday the hearers were summoned by a bell; and attendance was pretty general."[46] She continued, "The inhabitants lived in perfect harmony, holding most of their property in common."[47] Her judgment of her captors, "children of nature," was that of a much kinder, gentler people than the French jailers with whom she was later forced to face. She appreciated that the Native Americans shared their food even when "famine stares them in the face" and that they adopted the captives and called them "the tender name of brother."[48] (Her son, Sylvanus, was described earlier.)

Laurel Thatcher Ulrich, historian of early New England, credited the captives in northern New England as being real survivors. Some saw their captivity as a "spiritual quest for courage and faith," as Susanna Johnson did.[49] Others might have become Catholic under the influence of the French. Some older girls married into the Abenaki society rather than wait to be ransomed.

Sadly, one of the most brutal attacks in the French and Indian War was perpetrated by Major Rogers (a white man) and his men, including Iroquois and Stockbridge Indians, who pillaged St. Francis in the fall of 1759. He reported killing two hundred men, women and children and taking twenty captives (fifteen were later released). He burned the church described by Susanna and all the houses, even with people inside them. Two of his men became separated and were starving. Thus they felt justified in killing an Indian child for food. Further research on this point of Abenaki history revealed that Rogers only killed thirty Indians and that the Abenakis killed forty rangers, taking ten prisoners.[50] Yet the story was recounted with pride by patriots who thought that they had finally destroyed the Abenaki base in Canada.

Susanna's allegiances were definitely torn and confusing. Her religion was helpful in sorting out the heathen and the righteous, but her kind treatment by the Abenakis tempered her view very much. As she stated, she grew to have great "affection" for Sabatis, her brother, who "had a high sense of honor and good behavior, he was affable, good natured and polite."[51] Of course, there was intermarriage. Some of the first white male settlers chose Indian partners as stated in early town histories.[52]

BRITISH DOMINANCE

By 1760, the dynamics had changed in favor of the British. They built the Crown Point Military Road through the Green Mountains so a militia could mount attacks against the Abenakis. British settlers could also travel up the road. The road ran from Fort Number 4 in Charlestown, New Hampshire, to Crown Point over the mountains along an "Indian Path."

In his studies of Vermont, historian Colin Calloway verified that the Abenakis, Sokokis, Pennacooks, Shaghticokes and refugees from St. Francis lived "throughout the Champlain Valley."[53] The Sokokis lived on the upper Connecticut River in an area running from Northfield, Massachusetts, to Bellows Falls, Vermont. They inscribed the petroglyphs at Bellows Falls. Local historian Lyman Simpson Hayes described a "large ancient Indian town" in the Rockingham, Bellows Falls area, with hundreds of inhabitants.[54] By 1687, the Pennacooks had left Lake Winnipesaukee and relocated to Lake Champlain. Governor Andros of New York wanted Indians in his colony and urged them to leave their French allies and settle at Schaghticoke near the Hoosic River. Schaghticoke was a "melting pot" for various refugee bands, with many moving on to Canada or Vermont.[55] As the Indians moved north, they lived "among the rivers and lakes of northern Vermont and New Hampshire and had little need to go directly to the French mission villages."[56] On the western side of Vermont, "Missisquoi was a nerve center," and the Winooski Valley was a favorite location for hunting and planting crops.[57] The Missisquoi village was located in the present-day towns of Swanton and Highgate. Most accounts considered Lake Champlain as the boundary between the Iroquois of New York and the Abenakis of northern New England.

After contact, the Abenakis who refused to leave Vermont "became all but invisible to the whites among whom they now lived…they wore European-style clothing, used metal rather than stone tools, fought with guns rather than bows and arrows, emphasized the patrilineal transmission of important property, recognized distinctions of rank, were generally fluent in speaking a European Language [French], and had even adopted Christianity [Catholicism]."[58] Their native ways of fishing, hunting and smoking were all adopted by the British, so therefore they were "no longer distinctively native."[59]

After all, the area we now call Vermont was just a pawn in an international struggle between European nations. The explorer Robert de la Salle claimed the Ohio area for France, but Virginia fur traders wanted the French driven out and even joined with the Iroquois to push them back. The French were initially winning in this fourth major colonial war, lasting from 1754 to 1763. Yet with improved British leadership and neglect by the French royalty, the British began to win battles, with Quebec City being captured in 1759. The English had more people in North America, were better organized and used more advanced technology. The truce included freedom of religion in North America for the French, along with promised safety in remaining on their properties. All of Canada was then under British rule. British protection of the settlers in New England from the French was also now perceived to be unnecessary.

AMERICAN DOMINANCE

After the natives taught the British settlers how to adapt to North America, the British could survive without their help. It was then the natives who needed the British for trading. As the beavers became extinct, natives bought supplies with their land as collateral. Natives wanted the British "goods, guns, and alcohol."[60] Victory over the French in North America brought "migration, land speculation, and settlement in northern New England."[61] Between 1760 and 1774, seventy new towns were settled in Vermont. The non-Indian population of New England jumped from 60,000 to 150,000 after the French and Indian War ended.

The Abenakis still had chiefs, but their prestige had declined. Family bands existed with a decentralized political organization. The Abenakis rebuilt St. Francis but were under "the watchful eyes of the British, who were determined to control their relations with other Indian groups."[62] Since the Abenakis did not come to the aid of the French when Montreal fell to the British in 1760, they were to be rewarded and to "enjoy…rights and possessions and free exercise of…religion forever."[63] The Abenakis were to have lands west of the Green Mountains. Of course, those statements turned out to be empty promises.[64] The Abenakis did lease land near the Missisquoi River and reserved the right to farm there in 1765. The British Indian agents agreed that Abenakis had hunting and fishing rights but that "the land belonged to the king to dispose of as he saw fit."[65]

Indians in the nineteenth century moved between St. Regis, St. Francis and Missisquoi, according to Colin Calloway (St. Regis is presently Akwesasne, New York). Other Western Abenakis were dispersed from the

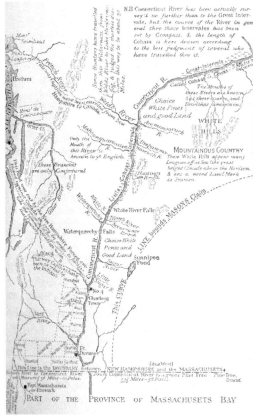

Left: Map of the Benning Wentworth grants, 1760–74. *From Edward Dan Collins's* A History of Vermont, Ginn and Company, *1903.*

Below: Missisquoi map showing Missisquoi Bay extending to Canada from Vermont; the Missisquoi National Wildlife Refuge is at the southern part of the bay. *Courtesy of the Missisquoi Historical Society Archives.*

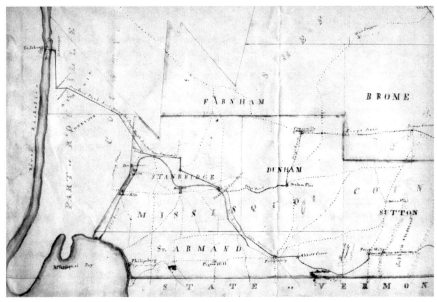

Champlain Valley to the White Mountains. Henry Tufts, an eyewitness living with Indians in 1772, estimated that three hundred Indians lived in settlements from Lake Memphremagog to Lake Umbagog. The British view was that St. Francis was the Abenaki base and any other bands of Indians were "wanderers."[66] Benning Wentworth, governor of New Hampshire, had issued a grant for 23,040 acres of land to be called Swanton in the Missisquoi area. Captain William Swanton had been an officer in the British army during the French and Indian War, and the town was named for him. That was a slap in the face of the Abenakis, who lived there and claimed the area as an ancestral homeland.

AMERICAN REVOLUTION AND FURTHER LOSSES FOR THE ABENAKIS

The American Revolution brought settlement in the New Hampshire grants (to be named Vermont) to a halt, and Abenakis were confused as to which side to support or whether to just be neutral. Ethan Allen courted them to join the Patriot cause with promises of blankets, tomahawks, knives and paint. That worked to a degree, with forty natives from St. Francis joining him for the invasion of Quebec in 1775. Yet other Native Americans fought with the British regulars to capture Ethan Allen in Quebec and occupy Grand Isle, with fighting in "skirmishes around Lake Champlain."[67] They helped the British defeat Benedict Arnold at the Battle of Valcour Island in 1776.

The natives tried to choose the possible winners, but they were not obvious at this point in history. The Patriots wanted the Indians to "settle on the upper Connecticut" as "a useful line of defense against enemies coming down the old war road" or as a buffer to keep the British out.[68] Many Abenakis from St. Francis had joined the enemy, General Burgoyne's British army. Most colonial settlers pulled back from Lake Champlain and the Otter Creek area in fear of the British and Indians. The 1780 raid on Royalton, Vermont, was rather bloodthirsty and, of course, had Patriots giving chase. Both redcoats and Patriots suspected the Abenakis of "subterfuge and espionage."[69] The focus was on the village of St. Francis, but Missisquoi Abenakis eventually aided the British side. The history of the Abenakis in the American Revolution is complicated, but the neutrality and then support for the Patriots did not help the Abenakis. "The American victory in their struggle for independence proved to be a major step in reducing the remaining western Abenakis to dependence."[70]

Two Indians remembered by some of the settlers were Joe Susapp and his wife, Molly. Perhaps that was because they did side with the American Patriots. Joe was a Micmac adopted by the Abenakis at St. Francis who scouted for Colonel Jacob Bayley, a British soldier, and Joe lived in Cowass Country, the upper Connecticut River Valley at Newbury, Vermont. When Bayley became a general for the Americans, Joe continued to scout for him, even helping with the Bayley-Hazen Military Road. Joe and Molly were located in 1792 at Hyde Park and received a grant from the State of Vermont from a local citizen. They were also documented as receiving grants in 1798 in Derby. After Molly's death in 1801, Joe moved to Newbury, where he was declared too aged and infirm to receive another grant. He died in 1819,

Hannah Handy being carried by an Indian raider urged to burn Royalton by the British in the American Revolutionary War. Hannah begged the Indians to leave several children behind in their drive to take captives. *Courtesy of the National Life Insurance Company.*

and when his grave site was no longer clearly marked, citizens asked the legislature to fund a new stone. In 1935, a stone with the words "the friendly Indian guide" was erected.[71]

Yet the American Revolution seemed to end the presence of Abenakis in Vermont in the eyes of the Republic of Vermont settlers. The old Indian village at Missisquoi could not be seen any longer. Joe and Molly Susapp had been observed as wanderers, even living in caves. Yet bands, not villages, were the core of the western Abenaki existence, and they did survive in Vermont, even though the Indians now had no rights to the land under the new owners and were considered seasonal visitors. Still, only a dozen families had moved to St. Francis. In 1783, Indians were observed on Stave Island in South Hero, Vermont. The settlers saw natives who spoke French, practiced the Catholic religion and seemed like "French Indians."[72]

Ironically, the Allen brothers, Ira and Ethan, formed the Onion River Land Company in 1773 and claimed the lands around the Missisquoi. In 1784, Ira purchased fifty-nine to sixty-four shares of Swanton land at a sheriff's sale and had the town surveyed.[73] Ira even declared that the Abenakis had forfeited any claims and had abandoned the lands. The court upheld his claim. Actually, the Abenakis ordered settlers off their lands in 1784, and Ira continued to protest to Canada that British Indians were asserting rights to his land in Swanton and Highgate in 1787. Even in 1790, fifty Indian cabins and cornfields were located at Swanton. Once Vermont joined the Union in 1791, "no transfers of Indian lands were valid without congressional approval."[74] Most Abenakis again pulled back to Canada. Still many lingered in northern Vermont and took to making baskets, birch-bark containers and trinkets to sell to the settlers.

Settlers knew that the Abenakis were there and often took pity on them. John Vincent, an Abenaki who had fought with the Americans in the Revolutionary War, petitioned the legislature for assistance in 1804 and received it. In the 1800s, "small groups of Abenakis congregated around St. Albans Bay, Swanton's Back Bay, the Highgate woods, the Georgia shore, Alburg, and the Lake Champlain Islands."[75] Their main hunting territory was the inland peninsula formed by the Missisquoi, Richelieu and St. Francis Rivers. Yet most Abenakis were perceived, at best, as part-time visitors to their camping grounds in the summer or, at worst, as gypsies wandering around and becoming day workers. Also, the Iroquois often claimed land in Vermont. Indians presented their land claims to the Vermont legislature in 1798, 1800, 1812, 1826, 1853 and 1874. The party line by the Vermont

This drawing depicts the joy of members of the Republic of Vermont who are now citizens of the American republic in 1791. *Courtesy of the National Life Insurance Company.*

government was that "those rights had been extinguished in previous treaties between other powers."[76] Yet "several hundred" Abenakis continued to survive in northwestern New England after 1800.[77] Some visited Bellows Falls and the petroglyphs.

Why did the Abenaki Native Americans not step forward to uncover this history and claim their part of the story as history was being written? Initially, there must have been fear of retaliation. After all, the Indians had a history of attacking settlers and taking captives. The Abenakis spoke their own language, or possibly French. One reason Gordon Day was so good at finding out the story was that he knew their language and could reconstruct their history from their oral tradition. Also, with the Treaty of Paris, the British had attempted to keep the colonists east of the Appalachian Mountains. With the success of the American Revolution, the Americans would determine the new lines of conquest and move where they wanted, even to the West.

Reverend Eleazar Wheelock decided to educate Indians from St. Francis and anywhere in northern New England at Dartmouth College, beginning in 1769 in Hanover, New Hampshire. The problem he had was that many did not want to take up farming, which was part of this college experience. They, of course, were to learn "the English tongue," and some did return to Canada to teach or preach.[78] The effort to educate Indians at Dartmouth largely failed.

As time progressed, the Abenakis might have been more confident about reappearing, but as Americans settled the west of North America and created Indian reservations, one might understand the reluctance to be a known Native American. Your fate might be life on a reservation. With the purchase of the Louisiana Territory in 1803, President Thomas Jefferson started to develop an Indian removal policy. After all, as historian Colin Callaway wrote, the planners assumed that the government "taking their lands forced Indians into a settled, agricultural, and 'civilized' way of life and was, therefore, good for them in the long run."[79] Indians should even be pushed by traders into debt so that they would give up their lands, it was thought. American settlements would surround them, explained Jefferson, and the Indians would sooner or later become acculturated citizens or, if they stayed in their culture, be removed beyond the Mississippi.

President Andrew Jackson, the famous Indian fighter, became president in 1828 and argued for Indian removal. He asked, "What good man would prefer a country covered with forests and ranged by a few thousand savages to our extensive republic studded with cities, towns and prosperous farms, embellished with all the improvements that art can devise or industry execute, occupied by more than 12 million happy people and filled with all the blessings of civilization, liberty and religion?"[80] In May 1830, Congress passed the Indian Removal Act so that all Indian tribes living east of the Mississippi were to be moved west. An Abenaki in Vermont would, of course, have chosen to relocate to Canada rather than risk removal to the West. However, it was noticed and reported in a local newspaper that in 1835, fifteen Abenakis encamped in Windsor, Vermont, with the goal of taking a native to Dartmouth College to enroll to study.[81] These Abenakis came from the eastern shore of Lake Champlain. So there was some freedom of movement and open appearance by the Indians, but in small numbers.

Native American Unsung Heroes

Native Americans did fight back and most of New England history focuses these battles, but there were also peaceful heroes who tried to represent their people with dignity and forbearance without violence.

Molly Ockett

Molly Ockett's life of hardship and adjustment is a fascinating tale of survival. She was born in a village on the upper Saco River in Maine in 1740, spending time in Vermont in her youth and in her sixties. Her life's story can only bring admiration and respect. Ockett's band was called Pigwacket for the name of her village, which meant "cleared place," but she was part of the Abenaki nation, the Algonquian-speaking tribe found in Vermont.[82] As she was growing up, her parents' band sided with the French to trade with them and convert to their religion as a protection against disease. In the view of her people, the British settlers were "all business, violating Wabanaki custom, which called for gift giving and friendly interaction in all dealings."[83] ("Wabanaki" was the "collective name given Algonquin-speaking tribes living near the North Atlantic coast.")[84]

After numerous battles with the British, Molly's father, in 1744, wanted peace and agreed to move to Rochester, Massachusetts, as requested by the British rulers. So the Indians left their village where they had planted corn and lived for decades. Her father and the warriors were to fight their earlier allies, the French. Molly, in her new setting, learned to "gather shellfish, sew, embroider clothing, and fashion baskets."[85]

Her family traveled in light birch-bark canoes. Then, in 1749, she was one of three Pigwacket girls to stay in Boston for about a year, and that was where she learned English, at age eight, and became familiar with another religion besides Catholicism.

Tensions mounted, the British declared war on her people and the natives left for Canada and Odanak, only to be sought out and exterminated in the Rogers raid. Molly survived, but not her parents. She lived with various bands in the forests of the St. Lawrence River Valley and Lake Champlain. In her twenties, she moved back to Fryeburg, Maine, married and had a child.

Molly was a "striking, large-framed woman…[with] angular features and royal bearing."[86] She wore a "loose cloth dress that hung just below

Above: Molly Ockett's birch-bark box.
Courtesy of the Bethel Historical Society, Bethel, Maine.

Left: Drawing of Molly Ockett, Danna B. Nickerson, artist. *Courtesy of the Bethel Historical Society, Bethel, Maine.*

her knees, red woolen leggings embroidered with dyed porcupine quills, and her traditional peaked cap decorated with glass trade beads."[87] She added earrings and bracelets to this notable outfit. She was "proud, stubborn, and independent" and known for her loquacious personality.[88] She was also skilled at hunting and trapping.

To survive, she learned about medicinal roots, used as "potions, salves, and poultices."[89] The early settlers did not have these remedies and were willing to try her cures since they witnessed successful recoveries with her potions. During the American Revolution, she sided with the Americans, but the increased settlement of Bethel, Maine, overwhelmed her. That was when she moved to the upper Missisquoi River in Troy, Vermont. Actually, her tribe numbered about seven hundred, living in settlements from "Lake Memphremagog to Lake Umbagog…some eighty miles."[90]

Once there, she and her neighboring settlers could barely survive. "To get by, they made and traded baskets and birch-bark cups and pails with several pioneer families who had moved there; but the settlers were also struggling, and the two groups weighed their difficulties against each other. When the white children came down with dysentery, Molly Ockett cured them but refused to reveal the secrets of her medicine."[91] The following year, when Molly was starving and sixty years old, she was saved by a large offering of pork from the settlers, and she did tell them her cure: concentrated tea from spruce bark. The hardships of Vermont still were too much for Molly, and she returned to Boston, where she had spent some time as a child.

After a short period, Molly left Boston for Rumford, Maine, and more wanderings. She offered her doctoring services in white communities, but they were "less and less tolerant of wayfaring Indians."[92] Even so, in 1810 she was taken in by the Hamlin family in Paris, Maine, and then with her magic powers healed their sick infant. Young Hannibal would grow up to be a governor and a U.S. vice president.

Even as an older woman, she "shifted with the seasons—hunting and gathering, roaming the region at will, and camping wherever she felt like it."[93] However, the troubled history between Indians and settlers was not forgotten. Some who sought her cures probably felt that this was a pact with the devil. Many felt that she had magical powers for good and evil.

In 1816, at nearly eighty, she was cared for in a wigwam in Andover, Maine, but was not near friends or relatives. She thought of herself as an original proprietor of Bethel, Maine. When she died there that year, stories abounded about her life, and many markers were posted. The legacy of her life is her bravery in adversity and kindness to strangers, even kindness to those whose ancestors had gravely wronged her people. More than fifty years after her death, a group of women from the Andover Congregational Church raised funds to add a tombstone to her grave as "Last of the Pigwackets."[94] In 1867, they were honoring her but also had decided that Indians were gone from New England. Her history was erased again. She was judged as the *last* of the natives in the area.

William Apess

There was at least one New England Indian who learned English and did speak up quite prominently to criticize how his ancestors had been treated in America. William Apess was born in 1798. His grandfather was white, married his grandmother of the Pequot tribe and gave birth to a son. That son was William's father. His father had married into the Pequot tribe as well. William was born in Colrain, Massachusetts, but he was raised by his grandparents and by other families in Connecticut. When older, he joined the militia, fought in the War of 1812 for the Americans against the British and participated in the Battle of Lake Champlain in 1814.[95] This took Apess to Burlington Harbor, Vermont, for an encampment of the American northern army of about five thousand men. He fought with Vermonters either on land or in ships on the lake. After an initial attack, the British withdrew to Canada. So the Americans, including Apess, had a taste of victory and the capture of some British vessels. In the 1820s, Apess decided to become a missionary and ministered to mixed groups of Africans and Native Americans. He was ordained as a Methodist and wrote his autobiography in 1829. He wrote and preached during the 1830s.

William Apess, a leading Pequot speaker, stood up and confronted an audience in Boston, detailing the oppression of natives in 1836. *Courtesy of the American Antiquarian Society.*

William Apess spoke out at the Odeon theater in Boston in 1836. He used the occasion to recount the history of colonial encroachment, beginning in 1614 with first contact. For example, the first explorers took thirty Indians to be sold as slaves to Spaniards. Apess asked:

> *How inhuman it was in those wretches, to come into a country where nature shone in beauty, spreading her wings over the vast continent, sheltering beneath her shades those natural sons of an almighty Being, that shone in grandeur and luster like the stars of the first magnitude in the heavenly world; whose virtues far surpassed their more enlightened foes, notwithstanding their pretended zeal for religion and virtue. How they could go to work to enslave a free people and call it religion is beyond the power of my imagination and outstrips the revelation of God's word.*[96]

His use of imagery and stern judgment must have shocked his audience at the time. To Apess, Metacomet, or King Philip, tried to get along with the settlers but was forced to "defend his people's rights and freedom."[97]

William Apess did articulate the issues of the times for Native Americans and made an excellent appeal for better treatment of blacks as well. Native

American expert Colin Calloway highlighted Apess as "one of the first Native American writers."[98] Apess's eloquence and desire to speak up for his native people is laudable and important to remember. Unfortunately, Apess struggled with the law and debts for the rest of his life and died in 1839.

Twentieth-Century History

In the twentieth century, many Abenakis tried to perpetuate their culture, but "poverty, prejudice and dependence on the white economy characterized their lives and promoted the tendency to conceal one's Indian identity."[99] Children who spoke the Algonquian language in school were punished. Thus, the treatment of Indians could be characterized as "dispossession, assimilation and neglect."[100]

Eugenics

In his book *Voice of the Dawn: An Autohistory of the Abenaki Nation*, Frederick Matthew Wiseman, a descendant of Abenakis, expressed his opinion that important modern scholars—namely Gordon Day, Colin Calloway, William A. Haviland and Marjory W. Power—thought that Vermont Abenakis "largely found their way to the St. Francis band."[101] He disputed this supposition that the Vermont natives had relocated to Canada. He believed that his "ancestors chose to stay and merge, in the eyes of the Anglo-Americans, with our French neighbors. Yet we kept our beliefs and customs."[102] Many became gypsies "who lived in upland environments, often in tarpaper shack shantytowns."[103] He described his view that the so-called gypsies lived in horse-drawn wagons. They made crafts or cut ice in the winter. "In the spring, the men would go fishing, collect ash or birchbark for crafts, work in the lumber industry or help their relatives with the maple syrup harvest."[104] Wiseman concluded that they presented themselves as Indians to tourists, gypsies to Vermonters and French to others.

It is somewhat ironic that the 1920s found Calvin Coolidge from Vermont in the White House as the president when Warren Harding died in 1923. No one really asked Calvin Coolidge about his genealogical roots, but if they had, he would have told them about his grandfather, Calvin Galusha Coolidge, whose mother "showed a marked trace of Indian blood."[105]

President Calvin Coolidge, born and raised in Plymouth, Vermont, in a Sioux Indian bonnet on a visit to Deadwood, South Dakota, where he was adopted by the tribe on August 17, 1927. Ten thousand were in attendance. Coolidge proudly accepted this, knowing that he had Abenaki relatives in his genealogy. In 1924, he and Congress made all Native Americans citizens. He documented his genealogy in his 1929 autobiography. *Courtesy of the Calvin Coolidge Presidential Library and Museum, Forbes Library, Northampton, Massachusetts.*

Coolidge never hid this fact and was rather proud of it, making sure that he wrote of his ancestors in his memoir in 1929. Since he had retired from office at the time of its publication, it did not really cause a stir.

In the 1920s, Vermont was seen as "the last great white hope" of New England by those who were fearful of immigrants coming to America.[106] There were many factors that converged to produce the well-documented intolerance of the era. First there was the domestic hygiene movement, which put a high priority on cleanliness and an organized household. A gypsy or nomadic tribe would run counter to that. They lived in camps without running water. Next, the influx of immigrants would encourage Yankees to hold on to their identity and seek rural outposts without as many of these foreigners, who were living in teeming cities. After World War I, isolationism grew in the country. Americans retrenched within their borders. Some Americans revived the Ku Klux Klan as a way to rally against immigrants and Catholics. The **KKK** did rally citizens in Vermont, with ten thousand attending a Montpelier gathering and five thousand attending in Morrisville. The **KKK** hate group wanted a "pure and Protestant" bastion. The Abenakis were not targeted as such, but if Catholic, they were considered "alien" to this group.

In 1928, Vermont created a Commission on Country Life to analyze the "social and spiritual condition" of the state.[107] Part of its study was led by Professor Harry Perkins of the University of Vermont, who wanted to see if "the science of human breeding" could help build a healthier society. Perkins was interested in eugenics as a "practical application of heredity to mankind."[108] The Vermont Commission on Country Life asserted that "Yankee Protestant tradition and heritage" should be a model for future community development.[109] The goal was to "protect" the "old Vermont stock" and prevent intermarriage with natives or French Canadians.

Professor Perkins and his social workers found 4,600 people with elements that "seem to encourage defectiveness, crime and pauperism."[110] He singled out "a hereditary degeneracy in large numbers of Vermont's rural French-Canadian and Abenaki populations."[111] With eugenics, "the drag of avoidable low grade Vermonters" could be gotten rid of if they were relegated to mental institutions and then sterilized.[112] The goal was to eliminate poverty and genetic disease. Perkins was judging who was unfit to reproduce. So he drafted a sterilization law that would provide prevention of propagation by consent.

The sterilization procedure would only apply to those "whose defects were clearly inherited and would complement special education and psychiatric clinics for problem children."[113] The law passed in March 1931, with case files now located at Vermont's Department of Public Welfare. Historian Nancy Gallagher's groundbreaking work on this topic reported twenty natives as being sterilized in 1946 at the Brandon Training School. So evidently it was a policy at some of the schools for "reform," and sterilization

Harry F. Perkins, eugenicist, 1921–25, professor at the University of Vermont. *Courtesy of the George H. Perkins Papers, University of Vermont Archives, Special Collections Department, University of Vermont Library.*

was a requirement if one wanted to be released from the school. The authors of *Freedom and Unity* assessed that two hundred sterilizations had been performed in Vermont; the law was in place until 1981. Eradicating gypsies meant that their children had to be taken away by social workers and enrolled in reform schools. The governor who signed the legislation believed that this would reduce poverty and reduce the need for government services since there would be no more children of the poor and disabled.[114]

Jeanne Brink, a modern Native American craftsperson and speaker, as recently as 2011 has pointed to the eugenics program at the University of Vermont as one of singling out Native Americans as "undesirable" and as candidates for sterilization.[115] Vermont senator Vincent Illuzzi revealed that in the early 1990s Native Americans spoke before his committee to explain that their grandparents had urged them to hide their background or "state officials [may] find out about it, [and] you may end up getting sterilized."[116] Illuzzi admitted that the state had pushed the Abenakis to "deny their past and deny their culture."[117]

Red Power

The Red Power movement (or the American Indian movement) was an outgrowth of the civil rights movement. In Vermont, the "beginnings of modern Abenaki struggle for recognition and respect" had begun.[118] Yet Wiseman, in his book *Reclaiming the Ancestors: Decolonizing a Taken Prehistory of the Far Northeast*, wrote that the scholarly community "controls the data and the theory."[119] Authorities saw Native American advocates as "emotional, dogmatic, or intellectually unprepared."[120] When the U.S. Regional Task Force recognized the Abenakis in Vermont in 1976 with documentation of aboriginal occupancy, Governor Salmon duly recognized the tribe, only to have the next governor, Richard Snelling, rescind this status. Even so, 983 people in Vermont checked the box of the census in 1980 that they were Native American.

In 1943, the federal wildlife refuge designation on the Missisquoi River took native hunting and fishing grounds away from the Abenakis. Those who lived there had to move out. This was a 6,642-acre refuge, including most of the Missisquoi River delta, where it flows into the bay. However, in 1979, Chief Homer St. Francis and others began the "fish-in" as a civil protest. In 1988, the chief demanded that the federal government leave the Missisquoi National Wildlife Refuge.[121] Under his leadership, his supporters staged more "fish-ins" to establish the title to the lands. They formed a tribal council, with a headquarters in Swanton. They hosted heritage celebrations and powwows. As anthropologist and Native American Margaret Bruchac explained, the natives taught language recovery classes and educational programs through the Title V Indian Education Office and in local schools, repatriated numerous ancestors, reclaimed some of the burial grounds on Monument Road and maintained a tribal office, retail store and museum.

In 1976, the Abenaki Self Help Association provided educational services to the community and obtained federal and state funds for the needy. The Abenakis who did live in Vermont were still not doing very well. In 1980, the high school dropout rate was 70 percent; less than 5 percent who stayed in school went on to college. Finally, federal assistance grants were developed for children and the elderly. Abenaki Acres, a low-income housing project, was built for all ethnic groups. In the 1990s, these improvements made a difference. Abenaki youth then had a 3 percent dropout rate, and 50 percent went on to college.[122] Yet the Abenakis were splintering, with four groups

Missisquoi River, location of traditional hunting grounds, made into a federal wildlife refuge in 1943; this moved the Abenakis living there out. *Courtesy of the Missisquoi River Basin Association.*

Homer St. Francis, chief of the St. Francis-Sokoki band, led "fish-ins" in 1978 and 1979 on the Missisquoi River near Swanton. His group wanted free fishing licenses and unlimited access to fishing spots. *From* A Vermont Century, Photographs and Essays from the Green Mountain State, *published by the* Rutland Herald.

in 1995 claiming to represent the Native Americans in the state. In 1999, the *Burlington Free Press* still opposed recognition since this "would lead to violence, gambling, a parasitic industry and development entirely out of scale with the host region. It might even lead to nuclear waste storage."[123]

In 1978, Richard Phillips and two other Abenaki men met in East Thetford to reestablish the Cowasuck Abenaki band.[124] This group created other bands that continue up to today.

In 1991, Abenaki community members in Swanton organized to save an area threatened by development. This was known as Grandma Lampman's land, about five hundred acres, where native people gathered herbs and berries and hunted. It contained sacred burial sites and was a place to "practice the Native Spirituality."[125] Martha Morits and John Lampman, both Abenakis, had built a house and barn there in the late 1800s. Their great-granddaughter, Louise Lampman-Larivee, shared their history as one of dancing, singing and storytelling. When it was to be developed, the family worked for three years against the "administrative bureaucracy of the state."[126]

John and Donna Moody of Norwich, Vermont, have spent years documenting and celebrating the history of the Abenakis in Vermont. John, as a tribal ethnologist, and Donna, as a repatriation coordinator, continue to educate Vermonters. Hundreds of thousands of Abenaki burial sites are unprotected, and the attitude of many in Vermont is, according to Donna, "outdated and destructive." The Moodys established a Winter Center for Indigenous Traditions to hold events and educate the public. Their Abenaki Language Project expanded in 2011. They also were advisors to the Vermont film being produced by Nora Jacobsen containing considerable material on this native history.

In 1989, a Vermont District Court judge ruled in favor of recognition of the Abenakis, but in 1992, the Vermont Supreme Court reversed the decision since claims were extinguished "by the increasing weight of history."[127] In 2006, the Vermont legislature did recognize the Abenaki people and created the Vermont Commission on Native American Affairs. In 2007, the Koesek band of Abenaki in the Connecticut River Valley appealed for federal recognition, and the Nulhegan band in northeastern Vermont appealed as well. In 2007, the Vermont attorney general's office opposed federal recognition of the Missisquoi tribe. The reasons centered on fear of land claims and gambling casinos. Finally, in 2011, a panel was organized to set up a process for state recognition of the Elnu Abenakis, based in Jamaica in southern Vermont, and the Nulhegan band of the Coosuk Abenaki nation, based in Brownington in northern Vermont.

Governor Peter Shumlin signed the two bills that had finally passed the legislature in 2011. The Nulhegan band has 260 members. Crafts can be sold as Native American made if granted approval by a federal crafts board. The Nulhegans are located along the waterways of Orleans and northern Essex Counties. The Elnu presence was proved with "archaeological evidence, historical documents; citations from numerous academic and local histories and oral traditions from families within the kinship group."[128] Tribes can apply for federal housing and education grants now. The chronology of native history in Vermont shows over 2,000 in the 2000 census as native, with 1,549 listed as Abenakis.

In 2011, Senator Vince Illuzzi admitted that Vermont had mistreated the Abenakis and that the past could not be undone, but now "people can

Above: Native American recognition at the statehouse, April 22, 2011. *Left to right*: Roger Longtoe, Elnu chief; Governor Peter Shumlin; Don Stevens, Nulhegan chief; and native expert Fred Wiseman. Photo by Luke Willard. *Courtesy of Diane McInerney, Division for Historic Preservation.*

Left: Melody Walker, an Abenaki from Highgate, Vermont, is now a citizen of the Elnu tribe. A living history demonstrator, she is doing traditional finger weaving here to make a sash. *Courtesy of Walker Brook.*

Left: Overhead view of twining by Vera Longtoe Sheehan; twined bags and baskets predate ash splint baskets. *Courtesy of Lina Longtoe Schulmeisters, Elnu Abenaki tribe.*

Below: Vera Longtoe Sheehan, a citizen of the Elnu Abenaki tribe, twining a quiver at the Native American Encampment Weekend, Lake Champlain Maritime Museum, Vergennes, Vermont, 2010. *Courtesy of Lina Longtoe Schulmeisters, Elnu Abenaki tribe.*

be informed about the history and cultures of Native Americans."[129] The craft of twining was continued by the Elnu band—they collect plant fibers and spin them to make cordage from which to twine bags. They also use red ochre, a paint that goes back five thousand years. There is now a Vermont Indigenous Alliance for the following tribes: Missisquoi, Nulhegan, Koasek and Elnu. The bands have cultural ties to each of the other bands.

FUTURE OF RECOGNITION

What can we learn from Abenaki history and settlement? We have been fortunate to have both Abenakis and Euro-Americans working at reconstructing the Abenaki past. This history is now being shared and discussed much more readily. At a Vermont history day in 2010, middle school students from one school attempted to trace the evidence of Abenaki presence in the state. Their exhibit shows the interest that students now have in this history.

This is becoming more and more relevant today as tribes are currently seeking recognition at the Vermont Statehouse. Native American Vermonters want their history recognized *today*.

CONCLUSION

Many descendants of the original Abenakis state that they are still inhabiting Vermont and want the recognition that they have waited so long to receive. One reason that their history has been neglected is that they cannot fit into the American national narrative of all peoples marching to liberty and justice because natives were done an injustice. Granted, the French and Indian attacks in the eighteenth century on the settlers and the taking of captives scared the victims at the time. Settlers wanted to remove the threat of Indians forever, not recognizing that many wanted to compromise and live and let live. Compromise was not in the vocabulary of these swashbuckling, larger-than-life early settlers, who cut down the forests and removed the stones to begin farming in Vermont.

Finding an unbiased account of early Native Americans in Vermont is difficult. After all, many historians and writers did not even think that Indians lived in Vermont in any period. According to them, Native Americans just passed through the state, and that was why land was available for Euro-Americans to farm. Historians such as Colin G. Calloway of Dartmouth College and anthropologists William A. Haviland and Marjory W. Power of the University of Vermont have changed this view. They revealed overwhelming evidence to support claims by natives that they lived in Vermont after the ice age receded, from about 9000 BC to the present. They recount the evidence in their books and articles.

Without a written language, Indians were voiceless in competition with the Euro-American settlers. They had to learn English and French to communicate. Most Indians were more comfortable with the French language and the Catholic region. This once again divided them from the British settlers coming in. Abenakis for the most part chose the wrong sides in war. They joined with the French against the British and then the British against the Americans. The winners usually write the ensuing history. Also, the Native Americans changed and adapted to the new goods being traded by the settlers. Thus they lost their self-sufficiency. There were more skirmishes with Chief Grey Lock leading the charge, but the Vermont government ignored the Indians and declared that they had abandoned their lands and therefore forfeited their claims. Small family bands persisted in traveling on the outskirts of Swanton, but for the most part most natives went underground or over ground to St. Francis in Canada.

The saddest chapter of the Native American saga took place in the 1920s and 1930s, when there was a backlash against immigrants and anyone who was non-Yankee (British-American stock). Those who believed in eugenics wanted to "improve" the Vermont population by targeting "the other" for sterilization. Inherited "defects" would be prevented with sterilization. The rationale for this policy was that there would be fewer poor people and not as much need for government services. Obviously, the Abenaki people in Vermont during these years would have gone underground or left the state.

With the civil rights movement of the 1960s, the Red Power movement swept across the United States. It took hold in Vermont, but scholars were the powerful ones in terms of data and history. Statistics on the Abenakis excelling were not good, though. In 1980, the high school dropout rate was 70 percent. It took Homer St. Francis and his supporters in 1979 to begin "fish-ins" to reassert Native American rights in the state. The next hurdle seemed to be "recognition," with the right to label their products and crafts, as well as gain assistance in housing and education. In 2011, Governor Peter Shumlin signed two bills granting recognition to two bands after a commission was set up to facilitate the process. This current success bodes well for the future and perhaps will mean a reconsideration of how history is portrayed in many textbooks.

PART II

AFRICAN AMERICANS CHOSE A STATE WITH A DIFFERENCE

Vermont's constitution was hammered out in Windsor in 1777, and it mainly expressed distrust of a strong government and urged governmental transparency. Every man, even without property, could vote. That was the first declaration of this principle in the fledging colonies. Also, Vermont's constitution banned slavery. Indentured servants were allowed to a certain age, but there was no lifetime of slavery.

As the historian Randolph Roth wrote, "Vermont's greatest asset was the character of its people—industrious, decent, courageous, fiercely independent, enlightened trying to enlighten the rest of humanity."[130] George Perkins Marsh, a Vermont environmentalist from the nineteenth century, also wrote, "In every good and noble undertaking, Vermonters would bring their influence for good to bear not only on the rest of the United States, but upon the world."[131] Vermonters felt that they were custodians of America's and the world's "moral, spiritual and political heritage."[132] So, Vermonters from the beginning of their fledging republic thought that they could forge a more democratic and fairer society than what they had seen so far. This pledge and then the history that ensued are the subject of this chapter.

The Vermont Constitution notes that "all men are born equally free and independent," becoming the most radical document in the English-speaking world in 1777. *Courtesy of the Vermont State Archives and Records Administration.*

LUCY TERRY PRINCE

Lucy Terry Prince, a former slave, moved to Guilford with her family but was harassed by neighbors. John and Amos Noyes cheated them out of money, beat her sons, tore down fences, destroyed their crops and committed violent and frightening assaults. She knew her rights, but a freed female slave in Vermont requesting assistance from the government was unheard of. Even so, she traveled to Norwich in 1785 to ask Governor Thomas Chittenden and his council for protection from her neighbor. Witnesses corroborated her story. The governor listened and then ordered the selectmen of Guilford to defend the Prince family. If the town did not help them, they would "fall upon the charity of the town."[133] Lucy was probably the first African American woman in Vermont to stand up for her rights as a citizen.

In another case, she also claimed the land in Sunderland that her husband was granted as an original proprietor and, when denied it, argued the appeal before the state supreme court in February 1803. Lucy, an excellent orator, argued and won her case against the two leading lawyers in the state. The court sided with the Prince family and gave them a financial settlement. Yet Lucy pressed for a place to live, and the town of Sunderland voted down helping "the negroes."[134] Lucy, then in her eighties, finally got a settlement in 1806 when the town bought the land originally designated for the Princes and gave it to Lucy and her heirs. Lucy had finally won her rights as a citizen.

She is also remembered as the first African American poet in America, predating Phyllis Wheatley. Lucy wrote "Bars Fight" as a ballad after an

Lucy Terry Prince, by Louise Minks. *Courtesy of Louis Minks.*

attack by Native Americans on two white families in Deerfield, Massachusetts, in 1746. It begins:

> *August 'twas the twenty fifth*
> *Seventeen hundred forty-six*
> *The Indians did in ambush lay*
> *Some very valiant men to slay*
> *The names of whom I'll not leave out*
> *Samuel Allen like a hero fought*
> *And though he was so brave and bold*
> *His face no more shall we behold.*[135]

When she died at the age of ninety-seven in 1821, Reverend Lemuel Haynes, a well-known black minister from Rutland, delivered the eulogy. Gretchen Holbrook Gerzina, Lucy's biographer, summed up her legacy as "one of the earliest and most important settlers in Vermont, white or black, and one of the most remarkable women in Vermont History."[136]

JEFFREY BRACE

In 2008, Poultney, Vermont citizens gathered to install a marker commemorating Jeffrey Brace's life in their town. Brace earned his freedom in the Revolutionary War and, in 1784, moved to Poultney, where he purchased land and married another former slave, Susannah Dublin. They were harassed by a neighbor, similar to the Princes' mistreatment, and moved to Georgia, Vermont. In 1810, Brace, then blind, recounted his life story before a white abolitionist lawyer, who had it published. It might be the first book published in St. Albans and one of a handful of autobiographies by slaves in Vermont. The memoir recounts his kidnaping from his home in Africa, the Middle Passage and life in slavery. The eyewitness account is riveting and has been published widely, with the original in the archives at the University of Vermont. The book includes this passage:

> *Now, although I am a poor, despised black wretch, in the sight of man, permit me, kind reader, to offer some ideas of mine, and do not despise them because they come from an African negro, who are, by white men, considered*

African Americans Chose a State with a Difference

Marker for Jeffrey Brace in Poultney, Vermont, with descendants. *Courtesy of the Poultney Historical Society, Poultney, Vermont.*

an inferior race of beings. I altho' thus considered of an inferior race, do hope, and verily believe, that I have received that blessing promised to those who have faith in God, and continue to the end in ways of well doing. Therefore, I have occasion to reflect upon the scriptures.[137]

LEMUEL HAYNES

Another important speaker and thinker of this early American history is Lemuel Haynes, who spoke at Lucy Terry Prince's funeral. He was the son of an African slave and a Scottish servant, born in Connecticut in 1753. Being abandoned by his parents, he was educated by a white family, who raised him in Granville, Massachusetts. He was treated well but still considered an indentured servant. He studied at the common school and learned Bible verses about the essential doctrines of grace. After studying Latin and Greek with tutors, he was given an exam by a group of ministers and granted ordination. In 1785, he was the first African American to be ordained by any religious denomination in the country.

He fought in the American Revolution and began to write poems about the war, appealing for immediate emancipation of blacks in America. His ballad about "The Battle of Lexington" contains these words, written shortly after the event in 1775:

> *For Liberty, each Freeman Strives,*
> *As it's a Gift of God*
> *And for it willing yield their Lives*
> *And Seal it with their Blood*
> *Thrice happy they who thus resign*
> *Into the peaceful Grave*
> *Much better there, in Death Confin'd*
> *Than a Surviving Slave*[138]

Haynes toured New England and even spent time with Reverend Samson Occom, the first Native American to publish his sermons and a narrative of his own life. Haynes was called to be the minister of a Congregational church in Rutland, Vermont, where he led religious revivals for thirty years. He filled the pews and built a strong, solid church. He had charisma. His sermons were popular and were distributed widely. Few, if any, in his congregation were black. After all, there were only about 250 blacks even living in the region.

He was chosen as the main speaker in Rutland for the twenty-fifth anniversary of American independence. He extorted his listeners to "destroy…distinctions among men that ought never to exist" since the Constitution mandated that "all men are born equally free and independent and have certain inherent unalienable rights."[139] But the main thrust of his speech was to praise George Washington, who, though a slaveholder, was willing to devote his talents to the public good and the value of a free republican government. He argued that slavery suppressed every principle

Reverend Lemuel Haynes, the first ordained African American in America. *Courtesy of the Rutland Historical Society.*

of manhood and that one should detest this "attack on the rights of men."[140] He explained that "union in every society is essential to its existence" and that discord was dangerous.[141] This was sixty years before the Civil War.

He also referred to Vermont, with its "peace, virtue and morality," as soon to "become a star of no small magnitude in the revolution."[142] Haynes's speech was distributed in the United States and abroad, not because it was given by a black American but because it was by a serious religious thinker of the early nineteenth century. He was allied with Jonathan Edwards in defending orthodox Calvinism and opposing Universalism. His sermons show that he was a significant black writer for his time period. In 1804, Middlebury College awarded him an honorary degree, the first ever given to an African American in this country, for his accomplishments.

FREE WILL BAPTIST CHARLES BOWLES
OF HUNTINGTON

Another minister who preached across color lines was Charles Bowles. Born in 1761 with African American heritage, he served in the American Revolution and then went out to sea as a ship's cook, but he settled down in Huntington in 1808 to live and preach for twenty years as a Free Will Baptist minister. As a figure in the Second Great Awakening, he led revivals, with participation by both races and both genders. Revivalists "believed in equality of all, regardless of race or gender."[143] Vermont's constitution allowed a right to worship "according to the dictates of their own consciences," thus opening the way for missionaries to convert the many willing souls. Bowles became known for his "noisy revival meetings" and "unblemished character and ability as a preacher."[144] Revivals were often set up as camp meetings, with many days of conversion activities.

Bowles was very successful, gaining many converts along the way. His favorite church was in Huntington, near Hinesburgh. Elise Guyette, in her book *Discovering Black Vermont*, characterized this particular area of Vermont as a "safe space," with friendship between both races. She concluded that "to have such a place in America was something few liberated blacks could have achieved at the time."[145] And Bowles enjoyed his grove in Huntington, where "away from manual and intellectual labor, his mind was free to soar aloft...[and to] give himself anew to the great Redeemer."[146]

ALEXANDER TWILIGHT

In 1823, Vermont was the first state to graduate an African American college student. This graduate then went on to be the first African American to serve in Vermont's state legislature and thus was first to serve in any state legislature. These two firsts for the state are quite remarkable. Alexander Twilight was his name. His parents were the "first Negroes" in Corinth, and his father had served in the Revolutionary War with the New Hampshire Regiment. Alexander was born in 1795 in Bradford but raised in Corinth as the third of six children in a state where he could be free as an African American.

His education began with a family taking an interest in him at a neighboring farm where he worked and at the Corinth District School.

Alexander Twilight, first African American college graduate in the country. *Courtesy of the Old Stone House Museum, Orleans County Historical Society, Brownington, Vermont.*

He learned from the *New England Primer* and the Bible. He also saved his money to enroll in Randolph's Orange County Grammar School at the age of twenty. He was one of sixty students studying to go to college or to become teachers. He took Greek, Latin and the natural sciences. In six years, he finished high school and the first two years of a college-level curriculum. Alexander then went back to Corinth to help build the first Congregational church and declared that he wanted to be a minister.

Alexander was encouraged by his friends to enroll at Middlebury College and actually met the president at his church. When he entered Middlebury, he was a junior. Alexander joined seventeen others in his class: nine to be ministers, six to be lawyers, one a teacher and two to make fortunes in business. Two years later, in 1823, he graduated.[147]

Alexander Twilight graduated into a tough world we can only imagine. He was one of 557 black Americans in Vermont. He found work as a teacher, probably in the Quaker community of Peru, New York. In those days, work for women and blacks meant doing something menial or teaching, at a different salary scale from their white male peers. He met Mercy Ladd Merrill, about ten years younger, a sister of a Middlebury graduate and a Caucasian. They married in 1826 and had no children of their own.

Of course, Alexander sought further education to better himself and make a difference in the world. He studied theology, earning a license from the Champlain Presbytery in Plattsburgh, New York. Then he could teach during the week and preach on weekends, drawing on multiple skills and increasing his income. He taught in Vergennes and preached in Waltham and Ferrisburgh.

A Middlebury graduate invited him to the "preceptorship" in Brownington. In 1829, he arrived in Brownington to become principal of the Orleans County Grammar School, supported by land rents of the county, and he was appointed the "Acting Pastor" of the Brownington Congregational Church. His students were boarded in homes around the village. They called him a "tough disciplinarian" with a "lively sense of humor" but most of all an "outstanding teacher."

Twilight wanted a new school, and when he failed to gain this, he convinced a local man to donate land. Twilight designed and built a massive four-story granite building as a dormitory and school. The building granite was brought from nearby fields, and Athenian Hall had been built by 1836. It is a bit similar to Painter Hall at Middlebury College.

The building stands today as the Orleans Historical Society. A visitor can see that on the first three floors there is a kitchen, a dining room, a music parlor, fourteen student dorm rooms and six recitation rooms. Each room has a fireplace, where live coals from the kitchen were carried to them in small iron pots each day when the school was in session. The third floor did not have fireplaces, but holes were made in the floor to capture the heat from below and were supplemented with wall stoves. The fourth floor consists of two classrooms, with a large assembly room and an iron stove. Wash water was collected from the roof in a huge underground cistern, and this was fed to the kitchen. There were sixty-five windows. Twilight had built the ideal school for his pupils.

Athenian Hall, built by Alexander Twilight for his boarding school. *Courtesy of the Old Stone House Museum, Orleans County Historical Society, Brownington, Vermont.*

Alexander Twilight's goal was to teach future teachers. Lectures were given in natural philosophy, chemistry, astronomy, history, moral science, geology, agriculture and botany. "Apparatus very extensive and efficient" is noted in the school catalogue. Students would attend a "religious meeting" on the Sabbath, with "difficult passages of the Scripture" discussed, with questions and answers by Principal Alexander Twilight.[148] An 1853 catalogue lists Miss Jerusha Tirrell as the teacher of French, painting and drawing. There were extra fees for her courses of study. In the summer, Alexander taught bookkeeping, accounting and architecture. Families would pay on a sliding scale based on the study. Tuition was $2.00 for common English; $3.00 for Latin, Greek, Italian, Spanish and higher English; $3.50 for written and spoken French; and $0.50 for vocal music. The hours were 9:00 a.m. to 7:00 p.m. Females made up about one-third of the student body.

There were some stellar graduates of Twilight's academy. James W. Strong was the first president of Carleton College in Minnesota; William Strong was the president of the Atchison, Topeka and Santa Fe Railroad; Portius Baxter was a member of Congress from Vermont; and Tyler Stewart was a U.S. consul to Spain.

In 1836, when the State of Vermont proposed to reduce funding for his school, Twilight ran for a seat in the state legislature to fight this and won his race. He then was the first African American ever to serve in a state legislature in our country. He didn't want the state to divide funding between the town of Craftsbury and his school. He argued that one good school was better than two not-so-good schools. He lost his fight since Craftsbury did receive the funds. Also, there was not to be another black person in the legislature for 112 more years.

His sermons reveal that he "regarded slavery as a relic of older civilizations and considered it to be out of place in a Christian democracy."[149] His words were, "[S]ubjugation by war and superiority of physical or intellectual strength never gave man the right to reduce his fellow man to his service without his own consent."[150] He continued, "From these practices of barbarism, ignorance and cruelty, arose our American slavery, so much detested now by enlightened nations, as knowledge has so much increased."[151] Yet he didn't become active in the abolitionist movement in Vermont.

In 1847, the Twilights had a disagreement with the trustees of the school and left to teach in Quebec. The school limped along and even closed for three terms. He was persuaded by the church leaders and school trustees to return. He was then the pastor for a year and continued to lead the school until 1855, when he had a stroke and then subsequently died two years later at age sixty-two.

The Brownington Cemetery adjoins the Congregational church, and the Twilights are in the first row. They were given a place of great honor. He was facing the school he led, the granite academy he built and the church he had inspired for many years. As author Howard Frank Mosher once wrote, "the Reverend Alexander Twilight: scholar, husband, teacher, preacher, legislator, father-away-from-home to nearly 3,000 boys and girls, an African American and a Vermonter of great vision."[152]

ABOLITIONISM

With the discussion in Congress about Missouri being admitted to the Union as a slave state in 1819, Vermont legislators introduced resolutions in the General Assembly to stop any extension of slavery. Legislators called slavery a "moral and political evil" and noted that any new state could not allow slaves.[153] In Bennington in 1828, William Lloyd Garrison published articles in the *Journal of the Times*, where he was the new editor. At first he endorsed the idea of setting up a colony in Africa for slaves who wanted to leave America. In 1829, he collected 2,352 signatures of Vermonters and sent this to Congress to gradually abolish slavery in the District of Columbia. He then returned to Boston, urging immediate abolition and began the *Liberator* newspaper. Congressman William Slade and Senator Benjamin Swift (both of Vermont) gave speeches against the rules that prevented the petitions from being read in Congress. Slade endorsed immediate emancipation on the House floor.

The famous black orator, Frederick Douglass, came to Vermont to stir up abolition. He was born into slavery, traveled to Baltimore and then escaped to New York and the North. In 1841, he began speaking in the North on the subject of slavery and was one of the most effective speakers of the movement for emancipation. He visited Middlebury and Ferrisburgh in 1843 to encourage those aiding runaway slaves. As historian Randolph Roth has written, Vermont "was home in the antebellum period to unsurpassed religious revivals and temperance crusades and to the strongest antislavery, anti-masonic, and free-soil sentiment in the nation."[154] Vermonters, especially in the upper valley near the Connecticut River, had one of the highest literacy rates in the world. Yet Douglass

African Americans Chose a State with a Difference

VOL. 1.   WILLIAM LLOYD GARRISON AND ISAAC KNAPP, PUBLISHERS.   **No. 1.**

BOSTON, MASSACHUSETTS.]   OUR COUNTRY IS THE WORLD—OUR COUNTRYMEN ARE MANKIND.   [SATURDAY, JANUARY 1, 1831.

Above: The Robinsons' copy of the first issue of *The Liberator*, published by William Lloyd Garrison, January 1, 1831, to appeal for immediate emancipation of all slaves in the United States. *Courtesy of the Rokeby Museum, Ferrisburgh, Vermont.*

Left: Mr. and Mrs. Rowland Robinson, abolitionists in Ferrisburgh, Vermont. *Courtesy of the Rokeby Museum, Ferrisburgh, Vermont.*

Top: Bench at Rokeby, the farm where slaves came to work. *Courtesy of the author.*

Above, left: Rowland Robinson and his Anti-Slavery Society books. *Courtesy of the Rokeby Museum, Ferrisburgh, Vermont.*

Above, right: Designation of Rokeby as a National Historic Landmark. *Courtesy of the author.*

saw the backlash to this movement as well. He wrote of "disrespect" in Middlebury, with few attending the meeting.[155]

Rokeby of Ferrisburgh was the homestead where Quaker abolitionists provided shelter for runaway slaves before the Civil War. Quaker church friends created safe havens for slaves there and at other farms in Ferrisburgh and the east Montpelier region.

Rowland Thomas Robinson, Rokeby's owner, was a leader in the Vermont Anti-Slavery Society (the state's first), begun in 1834, which produced a steady stream of printed materials describing the evils of slavery and which contained petitions for the federal government to take action. Ninety chapters, with over eight thousand members, had been created by 1837. He and his wife, Rachel, taught fugitives to read and write—skills they would need to start new lives. Louisiana runaways often hid on ships leaving New Orleans to emerge in Boston for travel up to Vermont. Most were destitute young males. Rachel Robinson once wrote to her sister that two of their fugitives could only stay one night at Rokeby on their way to Canada, "for they were afraid to remain anywhere within our glorious republic lest the chain of servitude should again bind soul and limb: poor men! They left wives behind, and deeply did appear to feel the separation…grief sat heavy on their hearts."[156] Slaves who reached Rokeby could venture out into the sunlight, far from their slave masters, who probably would never travel so far to reclaim their "property."

MARTIN FREEMAN DECIDES TO GO TO LIBERIA

There was another path open to freed blacks in Vermont. They could agree that a new country in Africa would be a better life decision than working on emancipation in the United States. Newly freed slaves and free blacks could join together to build a new world of equality. Martin Freeman was one to take another road.

Being a third-generation black Vermonter, Martin H. Freeman of Rutland was primed for success. Born in 1826, he was the grandson of a soldier in the American Revolution who had won his freedom with his participation.[157] Freeman was tutored by a local clergyman for entrance to Middlebury College in 1845. Of course, this was after Alexander Twilight's graduation many years before. In college, Freeman must have done very well, for he earned the rank of class salutatorian. However, another alumnus noted that none of his classmates would march next to him at their graduation. J.J.H. Gregory, a white student, remembered that he had responded to this cruelty by taking Freeman's arm in solidarity, and they would become lifelong friends.

In his academic career, Freeman was first asked to teach at the Allegheny Institute, one of the early black colleges in the nation and located near

Pittsburgh. This made Freeman the first black professor at any collegiate institution in the United States. He also was immersed in a world with college-educated, professional black citizens in Pittsburgh. Yet in the 1850s, the national political compromises with the South by the North were troubling for young blacks. Some began to call for emigration and exploration of the possibility of a colony in Africa. Freeman read Martin R. Delany's book, which argued that "blacks could achieve neither freedom nor equality in America no matter how hard they struggled; thus emigration was the only viable alternative."[158]

Martin Freeman from Rutland became the first African American professor at any collegiate institution in the United States. *Courtesy of the Rutland Historical Society.*

Almost daily, Freeman saw how blacks were mistreated in Pittsburgh and concluded that his enhanced status did not make him immune from physical assaults and racial insults. Obviously, his early life in Rutland was idyllic compared to the rough life of the city. He also wrote about his fear that intermarriage would be the only route for blacks to "be totally absorbed into the white population."[159]

In 1856, Freeman was appointed Avery College's president, but he was not pleased with the administrative duties. He married in 1857 and grew to believe that he and his wife should go to Africa and raise their children there so as to "bring up their children to be men and not creeping things."[160] Freeman learned about a new college in Monrovia, Liberia, called Liberia College. His American friends suggested that he teach mathematics and natural philosophy there. The school was funded by the New York Colonization Society. Once he decided to go there, he was encouraged to raise money in the States for his passage.

Evidently, he spoke in Vermont in 1863, but with the Civil War raging, many thought that a man of his caliber should stay in America since he would soon be needed to lead his race after the war. Yet in September 1864, Freeman and his family sailed off to "the land of their ancestors."[161] He did return to America for medical attention, but he reiterated his goal of teaching in Africa, where, in his words, "the Negro, pure, and simple as he exists in his native land, the best specimens of his race now to be found."[162] He never was comfortable in America, even in Vermont, where he could not recall a time when he was not aware of his "true status as a Negro."[163] Freeman returned to Liberia and taught there in the 1870s and 1880s, for twenty-five years, and was often president pro tem of the college, as the president traveled so much. On another medical leave, Freeman visited Vermont in 1887 and then went back to Liberia. In 1889, he became ill and died there. His family returned to Pittsburgh, leaving others to continue on with what he had considered "his duty to God and my race."[164]

Sister Eliza Healy

Another little-known educator was Eliza Healy, who was born into slavery in Macon, Georgia, in 1846, the daughter of a female slave and her master. She became a well-known educator in St. Albans, Vermont. Her path was an interesting one since her parents died in 1850, and she and her brothers were sent by the estate executors to New York to be cared for by her older brother. Eliza and her sister, Amanda, were baptized as Catholics in New York but sent to Notre Dame in St. John, Quebec. Healy finished her education in Montreal and then relocated to the Boston area. In 1874, she chose to become a nun at Notre Dame in Montreal and then to teach in Catholic schools in Ontario and Quebec.

In 1903, she was appointed the superior of Villa Barlow in St. Albans. At Villa Barlow, Eliza Healy worked on the budget to retire the debts and improve the school. Health and hygiene were top priorities. She was a role model for students and teachers until 1918, when she was transferred to Staten Island. She had been the first African American mother superior of a Catholic convent.

Delia Webster and Lewis Hayden: Stealing Slaves

Even though one would want to honor the memory of Delia Webster of Vergennes, Vermont, as the first white woman to be jailed for smuggling slaves out of Lexington, Kentucky, her behavior in the line of fire was inconsistent.

Delia was born to in Vergennes in 1817 and began teaching there at the age of twelve, which was common for young women in Vermont. She was raised in an antislavery area, near Rokeby, the farm of the Robinsons. She also attended Oberlin College for a while. Oberlin was the first college in America to teach blacks and women along with men, and it was a hotbed of abolitionism and a station on the Underground Railroad to harbor slaves escaping from the South.

Delia Webster left Oberlin to teach young ladies in Lexington, Kentucky. When Reverend Calvin Fairbank, a white Methodist minister and Oberlin graduate, came to town, he hatched a plan to rescue Lewis Hayden and his wife and son. Lewis Hayden was a slave rented out with a share of his earnings going to his master. He worked at the Phoenix Hotel and wanted freedom. One day, Fairbank and Webster hid the Haydens in a horse-drawn hack for the escape. Unfortunately, when one of their two horses died, the jig was up. They were discovered on their way back from successfully sending the Haydens on their way to safety in Canada. Webster's landlady in Lexington had searched her room while she was gone and found incriminating letters. Webster was then jailed and tried. At the trial, she pleaded not guilty and declared that she did not know the Haydens were in the carriage with them. She also stated that she was for sending blacks to Africa and was not an abolitionist. In other words, she was not willing to free blacks unless they were sent to Africa.

Back in Vermont, the citizens of Ferrisburgh met in a public meeting in 1844 and declared that Delia Webster had good character, and they urged the Kentucky governor to pardon her. She had been jailed in the Lexington penitentiary but was pardoned in a few weeks. Her father helped her in her defense; she declared that the North should not interfere with slavery. Slavery should be ended by laws created by the southern legislatures.

Returning to Vermont, she wrote a book with her father about her trial. When offered the opportunity to speak in public in 1845 at Boston's Tremont Temple, she did not do so. That is understandable since women rarely spoke to mixed-gender audiences. However, she was sitting on the podium and sold her book, which suggested that she did not "seduce slaves to run away, to be sure, but only counseled or aided such as were of themselves disposed to go."[165] She continued to teach in Vermont while living with her parents.

Delia Webster was not finished with the slavery issue. She claimed that she needed to leave Vermont for health reasons, and in Indiana she "labored among the colored people teaching them to read and write and also gave religious instructions."[166] She also bought land and started a farm in Kentucky. Newspapers reported that slaves went missing after she arrived and that strange steamboats landed nearby her farm at night. She was arrested again in 1853, jailed and threatened with punishment. Thus, she retreated to Madison, Indiana. She kept up her interests and lived with her sister and niece at times in Wisconsin and Iowa. She "did creditable paintings, writings and lectures. She was…an aristocratic spinster, giving lessons in the fine arts for a livelihood, not being able to realize her claim on the government for anti-slavery services."[167] She died at the age of eighty-six in Iowa in 1904.

Lewis Hayden was the slave rescued by Delia Webster even though she denied knowing that he was in the horse-drawn hack. He was an extremely important person in the lead up to the Civil War and during the war. Lewis helped John Brown with his plans to raid Harpers Ferry in 1859, urged John A. Andrews to run for governor of Massachusetts and suggested that he recruit black volunteers to fight in the Civil War. "Lewis Hayden was a principal recruiter for the Fifty-Fourth among Boston African Americans in early 1863."[168] His recruiting might have even brought him to Vermont.

After the war, he denounced white Masons for their discrimination and helped start black Masonic lodges. In Boston, he worked for integration in the schools, temperance and suffrage for women. He drummed up support for a monument for Crispus Attucks, the first man killed in the American Revolution who was also African American. (Attucks is honored with the monument for the Boston Massacre on the Boston Common.) At the event memorializing Attucks and the statue in 1888, Hayden said, "I am happy and ready to die now. They cannot take from us this record of history showing that we participated in the revolution to secure American liberty, as we have participated in every great movement in the best interests of the country since."[169] When Hayden died in Boston in 1889, all seats of the 1,200 available in the Charles Street AME Church were filled, and William Lloyd Garrison's son and suffrage leader Lucy Stone gave eulogies.

Delia had mixed feeling about her brazen act of smuggling Lewis Hayden, but her brave action to help him escape really did have crucial importance in the road of freedom for black Americans.

Thomas Waterman Wood: The Humanizing Artist

It is hard to believe now, but humanizing the image of African Americans was very important in the middle of the nineteenth century. To fight for black freedom, whites should care about them very much. As probably Vermont's most well-known portrait painter of the nineteenth century, Thomas Waterman Wood of Montpelier was not black but was very sympathetic to black Americans in his paintings. Born in 1823, he grew up in a family of cabinetmakers but was rarely exposed to artists who painted. However, his talent must have been recognized, and he went to study with Chester Harding, a portrait painter, in the 1840s. In the 1850s, he toured Europe and then began to paint portraits in Tennessee and Kentucky, eventually living in New York City, making yearly trips back to Vermont. During the Civil War, he painted *A Bit of History: The Contraband, the Recruit, and the Veteran*, which depicts a slave joining the Union army and then losing a leg in the war but returning as a proud veteran. His paintings told stories about reform with panels and/or with strong messages.

He was the first to "depict free blacks in contrast to the enslaved servants who had appeared as accessory figures in their masters' portraits."[170] Paul Worman, unpublished biographer of Wood, explained that probably the boy in the painting *White Rats with Boy* is a black Vermonter, but most African Americans Wood depicted were drawn from New York subjects or from his time in the South.[171] After the Civil

White Rats, painted in 1893 by Thomas Waterman Wood of a free African American boy with his pets in a sympathetic pose. *Courtesy of the T.W. Wood Gallery.*

War, Wood continued to paint subjects that represented "the American ideals that he saw as the country's foundation."[172] "He instilled Afro-Americans with the same dignity he bestowed on other subjects."[173] He chose a Vermont black man, his barber in Montpelier, for his 1877 *Man of Peace* and a white man for *Man of War*. In 1891, he painted a young black boy celebrating the Fourth of July. And as his fame and stature grew, these paintings would come to be known and to help gain respect for black Americans.

DRED SCOTT DECISION DEFIED

The Vermont legislature did defy the Dred Scott decision of the U.S. Supreme Court in 1858. In 1857, the court ruled in the case *Dred Scott v. Sandford* that "people of African descent could never be citizens of the United States."[174] The court interpreted the U.S. Constitution as relegating African Americans to "beings of an inferior order, and altogether unfit to associate with the white race, either in social or political relations."[175] The Vermont legislature countered, noting that "these extra-judicial

Effects of the Fugitive Slave Law, a drawing by Theodor Kaufman, 1850. Kaufman did enlist to serve in the navy and army in the Civil War. *Courtesy of the American Antiquarian Society.*

opinions of the Supreme Court of the United States are a dangerous usurpation of power, and have no binding authority upon Vermont, or the people of the United States."[176] The legislature enacted a bill so that no person could be considered property in Vermont and that every slave that entered would be set free.

Civil War Participation

Of the 709 free blacks in Vermont, 152 served in the Union forces. More than 70 of those men served in the Fifty-fourth Massachusetts Regiment. This was the famous black military regiment formed in Massachusetts to prove that black men could fight and fight valiantly. As historian Don Wickman recounted, "These volunteers were free men and often literate, well-educated, and from worthy professions."[177] Massachusetts's Governor Andrew and a military officer, Colonel Shaw, wanted to create a model "that would overcome the national prejudice against colored troops."[178]

Free black Vermonters did not have to serve in the war, so they voluntarily decided to join up. Perhaps black orator Frederick Douglass recruited many with his exhorting speeches:

> [A] *war undertaken and brazenly carried on for the perpetual enslavement of colored men, calls logically and loudly upon colored men to suppress it. Only a moderate share of sagacity was needed to see that the arm of the slave was the best defense against the slaveholder…Liberty won by white men would lack half its luster. Who would be free themselves must strike the blow. Better now to die free than live like slaves…this is your hour and mine…The iron gate of our prison stands half open. One gallant rush from the North will fling it wide open, while four millions of our brothers and sisters shall march out to liberty!*[179]

Since the federal government recruited and trained blacks, if a black Vermonter wanted to serve, he would join up with the Massachusetts Fifty-fourth and Fifty-fifth. Four-fifths of the Fifty-fourth were Northerners who had been free all their lives. Jeffrey Brace's grandson from St. Albans served with the Fifty-fourth. During most of the war, they could only have been servants or laborers for the Vermont troops. Yet by the end of the war, 14 percent of Vermont's blacks went to war in comparison to the

Frederick Douglass, the great orator and leader, spoke out on abolition, colonization, Reconstruction, lynching and women's rights. Born a slave in Maryland, he escaped to the North and became a speaker for the Massachusetts Anti-Slavery Society. *Courtesy of the Library of Congress.*

10 percent of the white male population. The most African Americans came from Rutland (20) and Woodstock (11).

When those blacks who enlisted did not receive the same pay as whites, they refused all payments for eighteen months. (The Militia Act of 1862 allotted $10.00 per month, with a clothing allowance of $3.50. The pay for white privates was $13.00 per month.) Their stand was effective, and they did win the equal pay eventually.

William Langley of Hinesburgh sent his three sons to join the Massachusetts Fifty-fourth: Newell, Lewis and Loudon. They joined up in Brattleboro to head to Boston, New York City and Folly Island, South Carolina. Loudon Langley wrote from the battlefront to the *Anglo-African Paper* of New York City and the *Burlington Free Press.* In February 1864, at the Battle of Olustee in Florida, the Fifty-fourth showed its mettle. As Langley wrote, they were ordered to retreat, losing ninety-seven men to wounds or death. He reported that the "rebs rent the air with cheer upon cheer," obviously relishing the defeat of African Americans on the Union side.[180]

If captured by Confederates, a black man's fate would be much worse than that of a white Union soldier. He might be killed outright, enslaved or

Campaign Sketches: The Baggage Train, a drawing by Winslow Homer of African American soldiers, 1863, for Louis Prang, Boston, Massachusetts. *Courtesy of the American Antiquarian Society.*

tried as a war criminal. Only after President Lincoln threatened to shoot a Rebel prisoner for every African American prisoner executed was the official Southern policy changed. Yet Andersonville prison existed, a place where death by disease, exposure or malnutrition could be your fate. Fifteen men from the Fifty-fourth landed there.

African Americans Chose a State with a Difference

George Hart, an ex-slave from Louisiana, traveled to Rutland with a soldier and then enlisted in 1863 and served with the Fifty-fourth Massachusetts Infantry. The photograph was taken in 1908 in Woodstock, where he worked as a mason. *Courtesy of the Woodstock Historical Society.*

Cast for the Shaw Memorial on the Boston Common, depicting the black Fifty-fourth Massachusetts Regiment. *Courtesy of the Saint-Gaudens National Historic Site, Cornish, New Hampshire.*

One private from the black regiment sent this marching song to the *Boston Transcript* in 1863:

> *So rally boys, rally, let us never mind the past,*
> *We had a hard road to travel but our day is coming fast,*
> *For God is for the right and we have no need to fear,*
> *The Union must be saved by the colored volunteer.*[181]

The regiment became part of the siege of Charleston, South Carolina. The men defended James Island and saved the "white 10th Connecticut Regiment from capture and destruction."[182] It was the attack on Fort Wagner on Morris Island where Colonel Robert Gould Shaw and half his men (about three hundred) were lost to the battle. Yet the newspapers in the Union states publicized that blacks fought and died "valiantly for a cause."[183]

In the last year of the Civil War, more African American soldiers enlisted, with fifteen black regiments in the Army of the James and twenty-three in the Army of the Potomac. Black troops fought in almost every campaign. Both the Fifty-fourth and Fifty-fifth Massachusetts Regiments included Vermonters who marched in victory in 1865 through the ruins of Charleston, South Carolina, to be cheered along by newly freed slaves. To quote one black soldier, "Cheers, blessings, prayers, and songs were heard on every side…the glory and the triumph of this hour may be imagined, but never be described. It was one of those occasions which happen but once in a lifetime, to be lived over in memory forever."[184]

AFTER THE CIVIL WAR

The Fifty-fourth received a glorious reception in Boston when it came north, but others from Vermont recovered in hospitals or decided to partake in the Reconstruction programs in the South. Loudon Langley of Hinesburgh had transferred to the South Carolina Thirty-third, USCT, in April 1864, and when he injured his back, he served as part of the field staff. When he was returned to civilian life in Beaufort in 1866, he saw an opportunity to be part of the rule over the South for a while. He even helped write a new constitution and argued that all schools should be open to all students "regardless of race or color."[185] He was overruled by the majority at the convention (sixty-seven blacks, fifty-eight whites). He wanted to protect the

American Citizens (To the Polls), 1867, by Thomas Waterman Wood, who is presenting a Yankee, an Irish immigrant and a German immigrant, all standing to vote, yet the African American is much more excited with his first voting experience. *Courtesy of the T.W. Wood Gallery.*

laboring man and those in rural and agricultural areas. In 1877, when the Union soldiers left the South, the black-run government was overthrown. Violence against blacks began, and militant vigilante groups upended the civil order. Loudon lost his house and moved to St. Helena Island to work as an assistant lighthouse keeper.

GEORGE WASHINGTON HENDERSON EXCELS

George Washington Henderson was the best-known black Virginian migrant to Vermont. He was born into slavery in 1850 in Virginia and was illiterate. During the Civil War, he was a servant to a Vermont infantry officer who brought him to Belvidere after the war. He was then educated at the academies of Underhill and Barre. He entered the University of Vermont and graduated first in his class in 1877, and he was the first African American in the country to be initiated into Phi Beta Kappa, the national honor society. He reached for more education when he earned a master of arts degree in 1880 and then a bachelors of divinity from Yale Divinity School in 1883. After his studies, he returned to Vermont to serve as the principal of the academies of Jericho and Craftsbury in addition to the Newport Graded School. Then he left the state for ministerial positions in New Orleans and to teach at the university level. In 1894, he was the author of the first formal protest against lynching in the United States. It was entitled "First Memorial Against Lynching," which he sent to the Louisiana legislature. He also revealed the legacy of the black soldiers in the Spanish-American War, some of whom served with Theodore Roosevelt on San Juan Hill in Cuba, by writing their history.

The University of Vermont honored Henderson with an honorary degree of doctor of divinity in 1896. The school recognized him as "standing in the front ranks of religious and scholarly men who are doing so much to promote the civilization and intellectual character of the country."[186] The Vermont Division for Historic Preservation has a roadside marker dedicated to his history in Belvidere.

George Washington Henderson, born a slave, went to school in Underhill and Barre. He graduated first in his class in 1877 at the University of Vermont. *Courtesy of Special Collections, Bailey/Howe Library at the University of Vermont.*

THE ANDERSONS BREAK BARRIERS

William Anderson left Virginia after the Civil War and, as a freed slave, also met a Union soldier returning home to Vermont and joined him. Anderson started farming and married Philomen Langlois, a Canadian immigrant of French and Indian heritage.

She gave birth to Marion Annette Anderson, on July 27, 1874, in Shoreham. Nettie, as Marion Annette was nicknamed, was a bright child ready for a first-rate education. When her parents heard of the Northfield Seminary for Young Ladies in Massachusetts, founded in 1879 for the education of those normally denied one, such as the poor and students of color, Nettie enrolled. And she flourished. She entered the diploma course, became the class president and wrote the class poem. Only half who attended would have gone on to college. But she did, becoming the first African American woman to attend Middlebury College in 1895 and the first in the nation to be inducted into the national honor society, Phi Beta Kappa.

Above: Marion Annette Anderson (first row, second from right), daughter of a slave, excelled at Northfield Seminary and at Middlebury, the first African American woman there in 1899 to become first in her class and the first given the Phi Beta Kappa key in the country. *Courtesy of the Northfield–Mount Herman Archives.*

Right: Marion Annette Anderson as a graduate of Northfield Seminary. *Courtesy of the Northfield–Mount Herman Archives.*

Commencement at Middlebury, a town holiday, was quite a day in 1899. The townspeople had seen male graduates of color in the past, about ten, but in the parade from the college to the Congregational church, the class valedictorian was a woman of color with a remarkable record of achievement. She had written the class ode, which they sang that day, and gave an address entitled "The Crown of Culture." Wearing her honor society key, she proudly accepted a cash prize from a Shoreham doctor, who had promised her this sum if she graduated at the head of her class. This she had done. The local newspaper never mentioned her race.[187] Nettie Anderson broke many barriers for women and blacks by obtaining these firsts.

After graduation, Nettie taught eighth grade in New Orleans for a year and then moved to Washington, D.C., to teach English grammar and history at Howard University. Upon her marriage to Walter Louis Smith, she stopped teaching. She probably helped her husband in his work as the principal of the Dunbar High School, the premier secondary school in the country for black students. They maintained homes in Washington and Shoreham, where she died at age forty-seven in 1922.

In her Northfield Seminary class poem, she compared herself to a daisy:

The sunshine of her life she gives
To everything around her,
Though brief the season that she lives
Nor lost is her endeavor.
She is indeed the eye of day,—
Gentle, hopeful, and sweet always,
She brightens many a weary way,
The cheerful little daisy.[188]

In a letter found in her family Bible, she also wrote, "I'd like to add some beauty to life—I don't exactly want to make people know more—but I'd love to make them have a pleasanter time because of me—to have some better joy or happy thought that would never have been experienced if I had not been born."[189]

Her brother, William John Anderson Jr., lived much longer and became a Vermont state legislator. He was the second black representative in the Vermont legislature, serving from 1945 to 1949. Will was an orchardist, or apple grower, in Shoreham. But his early life was similar to his sister's in that he attended Mount Herman Preparatory School in Massachusetts. The difference was that he returned to the school to manage the student laundry

William John Anderson Jr., the second African American to serve in the Vermont legislature, in 1945. *Courtesy of the Shoreham Historical Society.*

for many years and became active in the Republican Party, even attending Governor Coolidge's inaugural ceremonies in Boston in 1919. In 1920, he began his orchard business in Shoreham and, in 1935, was elected president of the Vermont Horticultural Society. He integrated the Masons in Vermont with a unanimous vote by all the lodges. Holding many offices in the town, he then was elected to the legislature.

Being a state legislator did not mean that all doors were open to him. Both the Montpelier Tavern and the Pavilion Hotel barred people of color, so he stayed at the Miller's Inn when in Montpelier. He was a Republican from a town of 965 people, so he was well known by the residents and he voted with them in mind. One newspaper reporter in 1947 judged his record as "brilliant."[190] When interviewed about being the only black person in the legislature, Will said, "I feel there is no such thing as social equality in any race. I feel as any other person feels, equal to my fellowman, superior to some, inferior to none. As time goes on, I am more and more impressed with the House. I believe it is a solid body that can be trusted and I feel that their judgment is right. I would not hesitate to place my trust in them."[191]

On a national scale, Will approached the U.S. senator from Vermont, Warren Austin, to work on the discrimination in the U.S. Army against black Americans. Will had served in World War I and was concerned about the small number of black officers. He urged that they consider a separate officers' training academy for blacks. A Senior ROTC unit was set up at Tuskegee University.

Will Anderson left the legislature and returned to his orchards but did not accept the new updated processes in his business and saw the enterprise become less and less productive. He became despondent and tried three times to take his own life. From one incident, in 1948, he lost his sight. Yet he continued to stay active and worked in the Shoreham Cooperative. When he died in 1959, the Congregational church was filled with people of various backgrounds and colors who were there to remember him as a man of community service. An article in a state paper in 1947 called Will "the Pride of Vermont" for his service as a state representative at age seventy-one.[192] When asked to go to an interracial conference in New York, he replied, "They'll argue learnedly about what the Negro wants, when all he wants is what any man wants."[193]

DAISY TURNER BECOMES A LEGEND

Daisy Turner was born in Grafton, Vermont, in 1883 as one of thirteen children, whom her parents, former slaves, nurtured. She did farm chores during the day, and evenings were spent reciting stories, poems and songs. As the history goes, Daisy's great-grandmother, an Englishwoman, was sailing near Africa when her boat sank. She was saved by a chieftain's son, whom she married. Their offspring was Alexander, Daisy's grandfather. He was captured and sold as a slave in the 1820s to a Virginia farmer. He married a Cherokee Indian, and in 1845 they had Alec Turner. He escaped from slavery in 1862 and fought with the First New Jersey Cavalry in the Civil War. He moved to Boston, worked in a sawmill, married and moved to Grafton, Vermont, in 1872. Daisy was born there eleven years later. She remembers the stories about the war, and at 104 she exhorted, "And these white people—how could I help but love them when they've given their blood for me? And as I said, the fields is fertile with their blood so that we could have our freedom and otherwise I would be a slave this minute, talking to you all."[194]

Daisy is remembered for her strong stand against racism in Vermont as a young child in 1890. As an eight-year-old, Daisy was singled out by her teacher to give a poem about a black doll at an upcoming end-of-year program; the rest of her classmates were given white dolls. They would present their program to parents and friends. Fighting back that night, Daisy wrote and delivered her own poem, noting that "half the world is nearly black as night. And it does no harm to take a chance and stay right in the fight."[195] Ironically, instead of losing the contest, she won it for her "original and honest presentation."[196] Daisy recounted this story many times to show how she faced her unusual position in a white state.

She never married, but she came close in 1923 when she was forty years old. She lived in Boston for a time and returned to Vermont to care for her dying father. After she returned to the city, her fiancé had an affair, and she broke off the engagement. She took him to court for "breach of an

Daisy Turner and her classmates (second from left, sitting on steps) and siblings. *Courtesy of the Vermont Folklife Center.*

agreement" and won a cash settlement of $3,000. Later, in Vermont, she ran a hunting lodge at Journey's End. When it burned down in 1962, she moved to the town of Grafton, and in 1985, she moved to Springfield. She even celebrated her 104th birthday in the Springfield Convalescent Center, with Governor Madeleine Kunin by her side. She had become a state treasure and the focus of study by the Vermont Folklife Center.

BUFFALO SOLDIERS IN VERMONT

Would Burlington be racially tolerant if a military regiment of black soldiers came to town? In 1909, the citizens of Burlington, Vermont, were concerned that one of four regular army black regiments known as the Buffalo Soldiers would overwhelm the mainly white city if stationed there. After all, the population of Burlington was 25,000, with only 117 blacks counted in the census. All of the state of Vermont only had 826 blacks at that time. The Tenth Cavalry would bring in 750 enlisted men and their families, as well as

The Tenth Cavalry (Buffalo Soldiers) was based in Burlington in 1910. *Courtesy of the Library of Congress.*

hangers on. Perhaps as many as 1,500 blacks would make much more of an impact than some were comfortable with.

The complaints were documented by the local newspapers. The editor of the *Burlington Free Press* was worried about racial incidents. Separate trolley cars were discussed. The editor of the *Rutland Daily Herald* wanted the men to stay at the fort and not frequent Burlington saloons. Yet the former mayor of Burlington, Lucius Bigelow, wrote in defense of the Tenth Cavalry as "gallant, courteous and kindly men, who make no trouble and merit no insult or derision from their white fellow citizens."[197]

Ironically, the men came back from the Philippines to a ticker tape parade in New York City before heading to Fort Ethan Allen, Vermont. They were heroes to many and "considered to be one of the best units in the army!"[198] Fear began when people heard about what had happened in Texas. A regiment of African Americans had terrorized a town, Brownsville, over a racial incident. But the Tenth arrived, and military discipline was a constant. Luckily, a small black business community decided to cater to the troops since some businesses in Burlington provided segregated areas or refused any service to them at all. Realistically, the numbers of blacks were not enough to "endanger white supremacy in Vermont," as the *Rutland Daily Herald* reported in August.[199]

The Buffalo Soldiers were on their best behavior, providing a regimental band to play for the public four times a week and arranging a benefit for the town library. Baseball games commenced with players at the University of Vermont and other Vermont towns, with as many as three hundred spectators. By July 1910, there was a patriotic parade when the Tenth left town for maneuvers. The Tenth also served as escorts for the funeral of General Oliver O. Howard. Howard had been a decorated white soldier in the Civil War, losing an arm from battle, and then he decided to further his service as the commissioner of the Freedmen's Bureau from 1865 to 1874. He had founded Howard University for African Americans in 1867 and served as its president from 1869 to 1874. He was not a Vermonter, but he lived the last part of his life in Burlington and died there.

The Tenth had traveled to other outposts and demonstrated new cavalry tactics for President Woodrow Wilson and his chief of staff, General Leonard Wood, who lauded the soldiers as representing the "colored race, and the eyes of all are upon it."[200] Shortly after this trip, the men returned to Fort Ethan Allen to prepare for service in Arizona, where they would chase down Mexican bandits. Vermont newspapers heralded the time with the Tenth as "very peaceable" with "courteous and gentlemanly conduct."[201] Burlington had appreciated the African American troops after all.

Tough Times

After the Civil War, times were tough for most people in Vermont up until World War II. Some historians call this the "winter of Vermont." As historian Jan Albers wrote about this time period, "In the years after 1860 the landscape reached its lowest point, as the state's fragile soils gave out, deforestation ran rampant, the economy struggled in the face of competition from the opening West, and the population was hard-pressed to maintain itself."[202] So it is not surprising that blacks left the state as well. Vermonters headed west or to the industrial factories in southern New England. Vermont was "the most rural state in the Union" in the 1870s and considered a "land of despair."[203] There was also a small social movement that targeted African Americans and Native Americans for discrimination and bullying.

The Ku Klux Klan and Eugenics

The Roaring Twenties featured a reprise of the Ku Klux Klan in the nation and in Vermont. The first Klan (deriving from the Greek word *kuklos*, meaning circle) rose up in the 1860s after the Civil War in the South to drive out carpetbaggers (Northerners trying to rule the South) and terrorize blacks to prevent them from voting. Now the Klan was rising from its ashes to promote "white purity" and harass and discriminate against immigrants, especially Catholics in Vermont. However, blacks in Vermont could hardly escape from the fiery rhetoric being bandied about in the northern New England states. The Klan in the mid-1920s controlled legislatures and the governors of six states, one being nearby Maine.

The Klan's goal was to "protect true Americans from Negroes, Catholics, Jews, social and sexual immorality, liquor and non-Anglo-Saxon 'foreigners' by promoting patriotism and Protestant Christianity."[204] A Klan member was required to be white and "strive for white supremacy."[205] Reverend Gilmore of Rochester, New Hampshire, spoke at Windsor in 1924, adding these words: "The Negro had a lower standard of morality than the white man."[206] Even so, the state was about 70 percent native-born Yankee, and the main fear was of French Canadians coming down from Canada. The eugenics studies did not approve of intermarriage among whites, Indians and blacks.[207] So, those desiring a pure Vermont and believers in eugenics did not include African Americans, while most white Vermonters ignored what was happening to blacks in the southern states and did not condemn the KKK.

Historian Maudean Neill studied the Klan in Vermont and wrote that it was active for about four years. He summed up its influence this way: "Many thousands of natives responded to the invitation of organizers, adopted the ten laws of the Klan and became its servants, existing for a season under its fiery cross. Other thousands, from their inner hilltops, resisted or rebuked the mysterious society, stood off, and watched it pass by."[208] The local papers in Vermont condemned the Klan at every opportunity, and that certainly made a difference. An editorial in the *Rutland Herald* noted that even if a person was born in Vermont, if he were a Catholic, Hebrew or black man, he could not join the Klan. It went on to explain that the Klan was founded on prejudice and "fosters bigotry and intolerance" and posts a "public danger" to society.[209] The *Windsor Vermont Journal* declared that the Vermont Constitution made provisions "so that all colors of skin and religious beliefs could live together under the protection of the law."[210]

Organizations "should never have the sole aim as to brand others as inferior to themselves."[211]

In Burlington, the city passed an ordinance in 1924 against wearing masks, which was a way to get at the Klan secrecy, and in Rutland there was a boycott of any business owner who openly belonged to the Klan. Yet there were cross burnings in Barnard, St. Johnsbury, Montpelier, on Lake Champlain and in Lyndon; a rally in South Royalton; KKK women met in Springfield; and KKK meetings were held in Milton, Barre, Windsor and Bethel. The film *Birth of the Nation* (with an outside female agitator) was shown in Montpelier. There was an open-air meeting in Morrisville and a Klan parade outside Montpelier in 1927. At the beginning of meetings of the KKK, all Catholics, Jews and blacks were asked to leave if they had dared to attend. So Vermont blacks could be worried about these meetings and the fiery oration singling them out.

The eugenics movement in Vermont focused on "fostering an awareness of the importance of good breeding," which meant replenishing "the good old Vermont stock"—that did not include African Americans.[212] This theory came from Harry Perkins at the University of Vermont in the 1920s and 1930s. His goal was to encourage "native stock" to stay in Vermont and propagate.[213] "Dubious studies on race and class differences" were used to "shape mental health programs and immigration policy."[214] Eugenics and sterilization would stamp out many bad traits, according to

The Ku Klux Klan parade in Montpelier, July 4, 1927. *Courtesy of the Vermont Historical Society.*

Perkins and his exhibit in 1931 at the University of Vermont. He wanted to prevent the birth of more children with feeblemindedness, insanity and predilection to alcoholism.

Critics charged that eugenics oppressed lower classes and minorities. When Hitler actually did establish a race hygiene program in 1933 with a goal of saving the Aryan race, eugenics began to be questioned in the United States. However, some advocates actually suggested using eugenics here to create a race to counter the Germans. Finally, a study by the American Neurological Association in 1934 found no scientific justification for eugenic sterilization. It took until 1939 for the formal condemnation by the American scientific community of Nazi eugenics. The Eugenics Survey in Vermont closed in 1936, and the sterilization law was repealed in 1981.

KAKE WALK AT THE UNIVERSITY OF VERMONT

The racism of the 1920s and 1930s did include the projects of Harry Perkins at the University of Vermont, but it could have been assumed with the end of World War II that any racist programs would have ended. However, a minstrel show as part of winter carnival traced its roots to 1888 and continued to be performed until 1969. A national culture encouraged touring blackface troupes, and they were often invited to perform in rural outposts, where the community wanted to feature nineteenth-century values and reject multiculturalism.[215] The Tunbridge Fair featured the shows, but most of these shows were popular in the South and Midwest.

The fraternities at the University of Vermont called their program the Kake Walk. This was a university-sponsored minstrel show! The show consisted of male performers in blackface walking about in a circle, taking turns in the middle with a special act. These shows had roots in the South, where originally black slaves performed for visitors to the plantation and characterized themselves as lazy and carefree and happy to be cared for on the plantation. Obviously the slave owners liked this positive presentation of slavery. As James W. Loewen, sociology professor at the University of Vermont, explained in his article on the subject, "The slave who was most comical won the prize, often a lump of sugar or cake."[216] The expression "that takes the cake" comes from this type of performance.[217]

After the Civil War and Reconstruction, minstrel shows came back and toured Vermont. In 1888, the Kake Walk show was part of the University

A minstrel show at the University of Vermont; these were performed from 1888 to 1969. *Courtesy of Special Collections, Bailey/Howe Library, the University of Vermont.*

of Vermont's fall celebration. In 1903, it was moved to February and winter carnival as a "central event of the school year."[218] After World War II, it was still part of popular culture to "demean African Americans."[219] From 1893 on, women were to view the show or usher, thus they were also considered to be supporters to the white males. Girls in blackface were added to Kake Walk as dolls in Raggedy Ann dresses ushering people to their seats. They were called "Nigger babies."[220]

In the 1950s, there finally was some protest against Kake Walk. The national NAACP complained, as did local alumni. The college newspaper criticized it. In the 1960s, there was more active condemnation with Bob Collier, president of the Inter Fraternity Council, stating in 1963, "If the Negro is being bombed in Alabama, then Blackface in Vermont is no longer a joke."[221] Kake Walk continued with a change in makeup to dark green. A black Vermonter wrote an op-ed piece in the *Brattleboro Reformer* newspaper in early 1969 complaining about Kake Walk, and this was picked up by the university's student paper. Still, in that year, the university was giving mixed messages on the subject. The president, Lyman S. Rowell, wrote alumni that he would not "remake the university" for the "benefit of Blacks" and end Kake Walk.[222] His director of admissions, Harold Collins, differed and was opposed to Kake Walk since it made it difficult to recruit students of color.

Finally, the student senate voted to end it in October 1969. It closed the curtain on the "last university-sanctioned event of its type," according to Willi Coleman, speaking in 2004 at an exhibit about Kake Walk at the Bailey/Howe Library at the university.[223] As Professor Loewen remarked in his article on the subject, "Kake Walk was culturally racist to its core." Whites were defining the images of "others." The "others" were "depicted with exaggerated, unflattering physical features and demeaning character traits."[224] The university was condoning a program that shaped assumptions about blacks that were demeaning. This minstrel show revealed a state university with a real paradox on race issues.

THE CIVIL RIGHTS ERA IN ONE OF THE WHITEST STATES

Vermont had only 519 blacks, or 0.1 percent of the state's population, but the state's attorney general wanted to go on record that public accommodations or hotels would be open to all. In 1955, Attorney General Robert T. Stafford "ruled that any public accommodation that discriminated on the basis of race, creed or color could not be listed in state-funded publications."[225] He was early to outlaw this type of discrimination. Massachusetts followed with

Attorney General Robert T. Stafford. *Courtesy of the Vermont Historical Society.*

a similar statute in 1957, but most states did nothing until the Civil Rights Act of 1964 took effect.

Of course, Vermont's Senator George Aiken made national headlines when he found a way to compromise in the debate over the Civil Rights Act. He felt that Title II would allow too much federal intrusion into private homes that were not large hotels. He wanted to let the local women who ran small boardinghouses with five rooms or less to "rent rooms to whomever they choose."[226] The compromise proposed by the Vermonter was accepted by southerners, and racially segregated public accommodations on a large scale in the nation were finally abolished. So

Aiken was helpful in finding this compromise with southern representatives in Congress and showed progressive national leadership by a Republican.

In 1964, Ted and Carol Seaver, white schoolteachers from Montpelier, decided to build a community center in the city of Jackson, Mississippi, "to serve as a base for activities to develop and strengthen local black leadership."[227] They did establish an integrated day care center and gained Vermont financial support for a while. Then they went on to focus on a Vermont fair housing law, with a proposal by Governor Phil Hoff in 1965 to not reject an applicant due to race. The Vermont Association of Realtor Boards opposed the bill, fearing that allowing blacks to move into a community would lower real estate values. Others said that Vermont would "destroy individual freedoms to correct a nonexistent problem."[228] Initially, the bill was defeated, but once a Human Rights Commission was added, as well as exemptions for owner-occupied housing accommodations, religious or educational accommodations or homes for the elderly, it passed.

BLACK TEENS VISIT THE STATE IN THE 1960S

Governor Hoff and Mayor John Lindsay designed the New York–Vermont Summer Youth Project. This arranged for New York City's Youth Services Agency to send youths to Vermont for six weeks during the summer of 1968 to promote "teenage integration through educational and recreational programs designed for young men and women of diverse environmental, cultural, and economic backgrounds."[229] Hoff felt that Vermont teens could learn about urban black culture, and minority youths could work in a rural environment. In May 1968, Vermonters were to lead in "conquering the guts of the problem, white racism."[230] The program ran for two years, but not without criticism. The project was supported by the legislative council but was discontinued with Governor Davis's administration. As a private project, it failed to attract funding and folded up.

IRASBURG INCIDENT

In 1968, Reverend David Lee Johnson, a black man from Seaside, California, moved to the Northeast Kingdom, to the town of Irasburg. He also brought a white woman, Barbara Lawrence, and her two children. For two weeks in July, all was going well, but nightriders fired shotgun blasts into his home, and Reverend Johnson returned the fire with his handgun. Local police identified Larry Conley of Glover, Vermont, as the suspect since he had yelled at black members of the New York–Vermont Summer Youth Project earlier in the day at Barton State Park. Police reluctantly arrested him, and when they did, the Orleans County state's attorney ruled the shooting a minor offense and fined Conley $500.

When a trooper assigned to protect Reverend Johnson found out that he was having an affair with the white Mrs. Lawrence, the couple was arrested at gunpoint and charged with adultery. State's Attorney Pearson wanted to press the case. Mrs. Lawrence was fined and told to move away. Reverend Johnson was threatened, and the local newspapers published detailed accounts. Eventually Reverend Johnson left the state.

The incident was a political football. Governor Hoff, after serving three terms, chose not to run again for governor. He had called out the "latent racism" he had witnessed in this incident and in the youth program.[231] A candidate for governor, Deane C. Davis of Montpelier, criticized Hoff for his remarks as not being "in the best interest of the Negro community nor of the people of Vermont."[232] Governor Hoff still appointed a three-person board of inquiry, which did conclude that "the police did not move as rapidly as they might have on the shooting episode, but moved with speed in perfecting the proof of the adultery charges."[233] The issue should not have been about the character of Reverend Johnson but about the "safety of a man's home in the State of Vermont."[234]

During Hoff's terms in office, he had helped lead the state to a more positive, multicultural place, with fair employment and fair housing acts and a student assistance corporation to help students afford college. Several groups formed in the 1960s to assist African Americans to achieve equality and security that was promised in the federal Civil Rights Act, such as the Human Rights Council of Vermont in Rutland and the National Association for the Advancement of Colored People in Burlington. There was also a statewide Vermont Civil Rights Union. There still were not many blacks in Vermont. When one African American did go to a meeting of the NAACP in Burlington in 1966, he looked for black faces and found none. What he did find was a group of whites who "wanted to make things right."[235]

HIPPIES FIND VERMONT THE BECKONING COUNTRY

With the arrival of thousands of hippies, or "back to the landers," in Vermont from 1967 to 1973, the state culture was bound to change. More than one hundred communes were developed with various philosophies and rules. Many of these young people thought that they could develop a separate society away from the Vietnam War and the draft. If they stayed longer term in Vermont, they "began to integrate into the towns and villages across the state."[236] The hippies were too radical for the Democratic Party, so they started the Liberty Union Party, which would eventually run Bernie Sanders for mayor of Burlington.

One commune, Free Vermont, wanted to help the urban revolutionary movement it saw in the making led by Black Panthers. Free Vermont created safe houses for Black Panthers and even helped them go to

Danny and Jesse, Vermont hippies, 1970–71. Photo by Rebecca Lepkoff. *Courtesy of the Vermont Center for Photography.*

Quebec if necessary.[237] Children of Black Panthers were sent to Vermont to attend the Red Paint collective school. Once the Federal Bureau of Investigation (FBI) and police started raiding Free Vermont, the group lost support.

Black Experience in Modern Times

In 1992, Louvenia Dorsey Bright of South Burlington was the first female African American to win a seat in the legislature, serving three terms. Dolores Sandoval ran for Congress on the Democratic ticket in 1990. Her great-great-grandmother was a slave on a plantation and was freed during the Civil War. Sandoval was a professor of education at the University of Vermont who spoke out against war and called for legalization of drugs. She was defeated by Bernie Sanders.

Presently, only one black legislator serves in Vermont's legislature. Randolph D. Brock III studied at Middlebury College and had a career at Fidelity Investments until 2003. Then he served as state auditor from 2005 to 2007, during which time he audited Medicaid for the state and found fraud in some state programs. He was elected to the state senate from Swanton in 2008, representing the Franklin District in northwestern Vermont. He looks to "root out fraud, waste, abuse and error in government programs."[238] He declared that he is running for governor in 2012.

The 2010 census shows that people of color exceed 10 percent of Burlington's population, with many being refugees from war-torn countries in Africa. Vermont, the second-whitest state in the nation, has more African Americans in jail per capita than any other state except Iowa. About 14 percent of black males in Vermont are in jail. The newspaper *Seven Days* found a bright spot with the University

Vermont senator Randy Brock, first African American male to run for a statewide office, the governorship, in 2012. *Courtesy of the Vermont State Archives and Records Administration.*

of Vermont, where students of color make up 12 percent of the freshman class and an antiracism group has formed on campus. The newspaper's editorial also suggested that more minorities sign up for state business in Burlington and that more should be recruited to work in the media. It also highlighted the Association of Africans Living in Vermont, an organization of two thousand refugees from twenty-nine countries who help one another on housing issues, language study, skills training, jobs with livable wages and the wellbeing of children. This sounds like a way to improve the life of Africans who have chosen to live in Vermont just as their earlier ancestors found a way to contribute through leadership in churches and schools and through their words and their writings.

Poet Major Jackson of the University of Vermont. *Courtesy of Major Jackson.*

Major Jackson is an award-winning poet teaching at the University of Vermont. When asked why he moved to the second-whitest state in the United States, he replied:

> *My Vermont is quaint comparative to My Philadelphia. Green in all the right places. I've yet to ponder seriously the move to Burlington, Vermont has made on my creative life. I mean: it's a stunningly beautiful place, with its challenges, of course. It's kind of a spiritual privilege to be here. I'm looking forward to writing poems about dreaming in green and noticing cyclical changes in the air.* [239]

Conclusion

Vermont was a state with many firsts for African Americans in the nation. Perhaps that began with its being the first state to write a constitution banning slavery. But the state could not ban racism, and it did rear its ugly head many times in the state's history. Yet the African Americans profiled in these pages did not let the color of their skin or their lack of education keep them down. They educated themselves, and they often challenged authority or the prevailing sentiments of the times.

There were also brave white people who defied the ire of their neighbors or the laws of the land. Delia Webster of Vergennes took the risk of smuggling blacks from the slave states to freedom, and she was captured and jailed. Rowland Robinson and his family at Rokeby in Ferrisburgh created a safe haven for escaped slaves. The artist Thomas Waterman Wood of Montpelier painted sympathetic views of African Americans in beautiful portraits that helped humanize a population that was often demonized in the nation. The Vermont legislature defied the Dred Scott decision with noncooperation.

And a high percentage of the black population of Vermont, small in number though they were, enlisted in the Union to fight when that was finally permitted in 1863. These were free men who went to the front willingly to right the wrongs of this country. Their participation was mainly in the Massachusetts Fifty-fourth since that was the black regiment that the federal government approved as a first step toward black soldiering. That may be why the Vermont black participation was lost to the overall narrative for so long. White regiments from Vermont were heralded far and wide, but black enlistment was overlooked until the 1990s and the research by historians Don Wickman and Jim Fuller.

Blacks coming to Vermont with Union soldiers provided another population of African Americans in the state. Men could get a fresh start in a new place. They and their children often excelled beyond what was imaginable at the time. George Washington Henderson, an illiterate ex-slave, went on to graduate first in his class at the University of Vermont in 1877. Marion Annette Anderson, daughter of a slave, born in Shoreham in 1874, studied to become the first African American woman to graduate from Middlebury College, was the class valedictorian and first African American woman to be inducted into the national honor society, Phi Beta Kappa.

After the Civil War, Vermont's population did not expand but rather experienced a tremendous exodus. Blacks struggled to hold on to the past successes they had gained. In the 1920s, they were targeted along with other immigrant groups by the KKK and the eugenics advocates. At the University of Vermont, it was considered acceptable to make fun of African Americans in a minstrel show called the Kake Walk, which was a high-profile winter event offered each year from 1888 to 1969.

It really took the late 1960s and early 1970s to see change in the Green Mountain State in terms of attitudes. With the appearance of the hippies coming to the state and the children of Yankees traveling outside the state, new views were being seen in rural and urban communities. A small black population appears to be evident in Burlington and near college campuses. In Burlington, the Association of Africans Living in Vermont is actively working to integrate Africans, mainly refugees, into the Vermont experiences so that once again, the cross-cultural experience can be a mostly positive one. Hopefully, most will eventually agree with the University of Vermont's poet, Major Jackson, who felt, "It's kind of a spiritual privilege to be here."[240]

Vermont has been "in the forefront of the struggle against slavery and for recognition of equal rights among men of different nationalities, colors and creeds."[241] This description of the history of African Americans in Vermont has born that out. So many of the stories of men and women show them reaching for citizenship and equal treatment. Yet Vermont is part of America and has often reflected national attitudes. As Howard Frank Mosher wrote in his book *A Stranger in the Kingdom*, "[O]ur Kingdom was a good but eminently improvable place, where the past was still part of the present."[242] The history of Vermont should include the stories of African Americans to complete the narrative and enrich it for us all.

NATIONAL AND STATE FIRST-TIME SUCCESSES FOR AFRICAN AMERICANS IN VERMONT

1746: Lucy Terry Prince writes "Bars Fight" and is the first female African American poet in the country.

1775: Lemuel Haynes writes poems and a ballad, "The Battle of Lexington."

1777: Vermont is the first state to ban slavery in its constitution.

1785: Lucy Terry Prince, a freed slave, testifies before the governor of Vermont, Thomas Chittenden, for protection from her neighbor and wins. She is probably the first African American woman in the country to appeal for her rights before a governor of a state.

1785: Lemuel Haynes is the first African American to be ordained by any religious denomination, in Connecticut, and he goes to serve as a minister in Rutland, Vermont. He is the first black man to write antislavery literature, but it is unpublished.

1803: Lucy Terry Prince appeals before the Vermont Supreme Court for her land grant in Sunderland and wins.

1804: Middlebury College, Vermont, awards Lemuel Haynes an honorary degree, the first ever given to an African American in this country.

1810: Jeffrey Brace writes and publishes his autobiography about his life as a slave; this is probably the first book published in St. Albans, Vermont, and a rare autobiography by a former slave.

1823: Alexander Twilight is the first African American to graduate from a college in this country, at Middlebury College.

1836: Alexander Twilight wins a seat in the Vermont legislature to become the first black person to serve in a state legislature in our country.

1840s: Martin Freeman of Rutland is the first black professor at any collegiate institution in the United States, at Allegheny Institute in Pittsburgh, Pennsylvania.

1863: Free Vermont blacks enlist to fight in the Civil War—14 percent of the Vermont black population.

1877: George Washington Henderson is the first African American in the country to be initiated into Phi Beta Kappa, the national honor society, and he graduates first in his class at the University of Vermont.

1894: George Washington Henderson writes the first formal protest against lynching in the United States when in Louisiana and sends it to the state legislature.

1895: Marion Annette Anderson is the first African American woman to attend Middlebury College and, in 1899, is the first African American woman in the nation to be inducted into Phi Beta Kappa.

1903: Sister Eliza Healy is appointed mother superior of a Catholic convent in St. Albans, the first African American woman to achieve this status in the Catholic Church in America.

1945: William John Anderson Jr., brother of Marion Annette Anderson, is the second African American to serve in the Vermont legislature.

1990: Dolores Sandoval is the first African American female to run for a statewide office in Vermont. She runs for Congress on the Democratic ticket but loses to Bernie Sanders (as an independent).

1992: Louvenia Dorsey Bright of South Burlington is the first female African American to serve in the Vermont legislature.

2008: Vermont is the first state to be declared for Barack Obama in the election of 2008.

2012: State senator Randy Brock declares himself a candidate for governor. He is the first African American male to run for a statewide office in the state.

PART III

WOMEN'S HISTORY

The Other Half of the Story

Women, the nurturers of children and families, often did not appear prominently in narratives of early Vermont history since they were not warriors. They were busy with home life and food preparation. In the early days of Vermont history, women had many children, and that was their primary responsibility. The men were to help provide for the family with hunting and home building. This could be said for both natives and the English settlers. Yet the story of women and their contributions should be told. After all, they are half the history and make up half the population of Vermont.

NATIVE AMERICAN WOMEN IN VERMONT

In the Woodland period, about 2970 BC, agriculture became important to the natives in Vermont. They grew squash, gourds, maize and beans from seeds that they received from trading with southern tribes. In addition, local sunflowers, marsh elder and chenopodium were also cultivated. Women gathered the acorns, beechnuts, chestnuts, berries, leaves, roots, seeds and flowers. They cut maple trees for the sweet sap and collected it. Pottery and soapstone bowls were used. Since ceramics and chipped stone tools were found on the Winooski River near Lake Champlain, researchers have concluded that there was seasonal living there, with butternuts and fish as the main food and with hunting, gathering and fishing as the way of life. Basket making "was the primary mode of artistic expression for many… [it] was considered women's work."[243] This took much time and became an art. Even before making the basket, a woman first gathered, prepared and sorted her supplies, with little girls learning this art at the knee of a mother or grandmother.

Of course, we know more about Native American women once they made contact with Europeans. Observers could only tell us what they knew since natives did not speak English, at least initially. Fur trade with Europeans disrupted women's roles in the home village and in farming. They were now valued for "dressing the fur pelts."[244] In some ways, they did not alter their materials due to European influence as fast as their men did. Men wanted to use metal, but women kept making pottery and carried a tool kit of stone, wood and bone. Pottery was made by hand, not at a potter's wheel. Bark containers were important for light travel. Women made maple sugar and sold feathers as part of the Atlantic trading network. Women pounded,

Archaic Indian hunting party, with women and children preparing the animal. *Courtesy of the New York State Museum, Albany, New York.*

dried, packed and stored cornmeal for winter. They also set up and pulled down each temporary village. European observers felt that women had much more work than their men did. Still, women took time out to swim, even taking their children on their backs along with them. They also "participated in riding, horse racing, foot racing and snow sledding."[245] So they may have worked hard but also had enjoyment.

Females wore "breechclout and belt...with a knee length skirt of tanned buckskin."[246] They favored long hair, either braided or loose, with a headband or in a crown on their heads. In the 1770s, one observer described a native woman with "nose and ear jewels, and bracelets on her arms; besides a variety of trinkets and gewgaws decorating the other parts of her body."[247] The art of using porcupine quills and beads to make clothing "demanded delicate dexterity and well-developed skill."[248] Beadwork became quite an art, with tiny glass beads obtained in trade. "Indians made beads out of shell, stone, deer hooves, animal teeth, bones, nuts, seeds, and shiny or brilliantly colored stones."[249] They loved the colorful cloth from the Europeans.

Women had "a large degree of authority within the clan."[250] Living patterns centered on households of one to four nuclear families in a single structure. They could choose to locate with the husband or wife's family, and each family band had a designated hunting area. If a group became too numerous, a newly married couple could join the other spouse's family band.

Infants were placed on cradle boards. If they did not survive, they were considered unfit to care for themselves in the "other world" and friends would offer gifts to the parents in grief.[251] Native children were raised fairly permissively but told morality tales. Female children were tutored in child rearing and how to make clothing and beadwork.

Marriage was with those outside your family band but in your "major band."[252] After gifts from a suitor, a woman could enter a trial period of living with a man, but sleeping head to foot, and the woman could reject the proposal. If a man was accepted, the family would feast and dance for the occasion. Life expectancy was similar to that of Europeans, about thirty-seven years old, but any woman who survived the childbearing years had a shot at growing old. Rape was considered a "gross sexual violation and was widely condemned among Native Americans."[253] This extended to white captives as well.

Death meant burial immediately to send the spirits away. The deceased was well dressed and given utensils for his or her journey, with the family band mourning at a graveside ceremony. Women were the "chief mourners," and

Indian Family, a print by G. Gleason, 1844–49, from a lithograph by Currier, showing a family unit at work and a mother nursing her infant. *Courtesy of the American Antiquarian Society.*

wailing was important. "It was a chance for all the participants to give vent to their accumulated grief and sadness."[254] Widows spent a year in mourning, wearing a hood and staying away from social life. Widowers were also to be restrained for a year by staying out of social life and not marrying.

Shamans had "considerable measure of control over the spirit world."[255] Shamans could be men or women who purported to see the future. They could suggest tracks to find game and concoct cures for illnesses. Employing a cedar flute and drums, they called forth game and lured enemies into traps. Yet there was reverence for animals and respect for living things. A social order existed, with designated acceptable behavior consisting of a "fear of the supernatural and direct retaliation."[256] Religion was "a ceaseless conversation with the creator of all things."[257] Women "lived in a world of mysticism and symbolism where every part of the earth and heavens possessed a spiritual life."[258] Ceremonies helped focus their way of life. Girls and boys were to seek spiritual helpers. Women were to be part of religious rituals "with prayers for a sufficient food supply [and] good health for tribal members."[259]

Since women were responsible for daily life, they were "conservators of culture in the context of crisis."[260] Older women gained more respect as they lived longer. Their opinions mattered more, and they were "consulted regarding herbal medicines, sacred matters, and tribal history."[261] Grandmothers passed on the values and wisdom of the tribe to their grandchildren. "Life held few surprises for the typical early Native American woman. Surrounded by women at birth, she continued her life in the presence and company of women, sharing with the sisters of her tribe her learning, her working, her own labors of childbirth, and her death."[262] In contrast to some modern women, she knew her identity.

Historians and anthropologists believe that "the Indian woman generally enjoyed a good deal more independence and security than the white woman."[263] The tribe would provide for the native woman; a white woman who lost her husband might have to look for a poor farm.

How were the natives viewed by the early settlers? Vermont writer Dorothy Canfield Fisher, looking back at this history from her view in 1953, claimed that there was toleration and admiration but then described them as a "few stray Indian hunters who, with their strong smelling wives and dirty, bright-eyed children, occasionally came padding on their moccasined feet down the Green Mountain trails into the settlements."[264] She concluded, "Racial minorities, if they are small enough and do not threaten economic competition, are always fairly safe from mass prejudice."[265]

EARLY SETTLERS FROM EUROPEAN ROOTS

Dorothy Canfield Fisher, herself a descendant from early British settlers of Arlington, Vermont, also characterized the white female settlers of the state as deciding on their own to leave comfortable homes in Connecticut and Massachusetts and not being dominated at all by their men. Laurel Thatcher Ulrich, the Harvard professor and scholar of women's studies, noted that "tales about pioneer women as courageous and powerful as Molly [Ockett] gave white settlers a claim on the land."[266] They felt that they deserved the land since they had tamed it and conquered the Indians. Their God wanted them to dominate nature and the land. For example, Ann Story came to Salisbury, Vermont, in 1775 with her husband and five children. She was a helper to the Green Mountain Boys when she stood up against the claims on the land by the New York sheriffs and hid her family from the Indian raiders.

But most studies of the era document the legal and social realities of women, who were dominated legally by patriarchy and religious beliefs. Women knew that they were inferior by their community's interpretation of the Bible and their legal rights. A married woman was "covered" by her husband since "she had no independent legal standing."[267] A woman could not own property, sign a contract, keep her wages if her husband wanted them or keep anything more than her clothes. Her children were not hers alone and would reside with her husband if there was a separation. If all went well, the security of a husband or father was a blessing. The male of each household was to "protect, support, and represent" the females.[268] If this went asunder, a woman had no rights in a marriage gone awry. Only if a woman was single or a widow could she own property and make contracts.

Early life in the first areas settled by whites in Vermont would have meant living in one room with a large fireplace for heat and food preparation. Ironically, for both natives and the new settlers, women's work was to be focused on maintaining the fire and cooking food for the family. The first homesteaders ate off pine planks without plates or utensils and often ate a meal from a common bowl.

Education, then, was an important step for women. Vermont was unusual, offering schools for all. Most New England women had not had much formal education and might even have been "bound out" to other families as servants, during which time they might learn to read.[269] Once married, women were placed into a "cycle of pregnancy, birth, and breast-feeding that recurred every two to three years."[270] The average family had about eight children, but of course not all would live and thrive.

Early settlers cooking. *Courtesy of the National Life Insurance Company.*

One example of this system of patriarchy is the use of the word "relict," which means widow; to put that on a tombstone could be considered demeaning. A woman was only remembered through her connection to her husband. Also, "relict" means an inferior person, not even worthy of having her own maiden name on a tombstone. Tombstones never recorded maiden names. "As their husbands' vassals, even in death, women were deprived of their family origins and familial identity."[271] The following is an example from the Brattleboro cemetery:

> *Experience*
> *Relict of Samuel Wellington*
> *Died Dec. 17, 1838*
> *Age 69*
> *Her first husband was Elias Bemis*[272]

A young woman reading in a one-room school. *Courtesy of the National Life Insurance Company.*

So Experience was twice a relict and never given a maiden name. This also makes it difficult to trace genealogy for women. Relicts would then preside over the "dissolution of a family," meaning that a widow would obtain property determined by the court or her husband's will.[273] She might have to move in with relatives, so great instability developed with the death of her husband.

In Vermont cemeteries, there are rows of small graves, often next to a grave for a young mother. Childbearing was a brave business that you might not survive. Doctors who helped often inadvertently gave women infections that could kill them. Then again, the infants might not survive, and if they did, epidemics of "smallpox, measles, diphtheria, scarlet fever, and tuberculosis" might take many children in the family.[274]

One historian who has pieced together early women's history is Laurel Thatcher Ulrich. Her book *A Midwife's Tale: The Life of Martha Ballard, Based on Her Diary, 1785–1812* won a Pulitzer Prize. The diary Ulrich interpreted was rejected as uninteresting by male historians for years, but this female historian pieced together the story of domestic life in Hallowell, Maine. Martha Ballard was a midwife who delivered 816 babies in twenty-seven years and gave birth to 9 children of her own.

The daily life of women in this era was re-created by Ulrich's interpretation of this diary, and her work opened up a world of women's history that can never be closed again. Ulrich looked for "evidence of female life lay buried in sermons, account books, probate inventories, genealogies, church records, court records, paintings, embroideries, gravestones and the private papers of husbands and sons."[275] She used "role analysis" to re-create the daily lives of these early colonial women.[276] She also listed the roles that a woman might have: housewife, deputy husband, consort, mother, mistress, neighbor and Christian. A consort "tuned her life to her mate's."[277] A mistress served others by training young women to take over her roles some day. A Christian "seized spiritual equality and remained silent in church."[278] Church membership was the one public membership that most women could achieve. Women, with their multiple roles, worked hard to settle towns in the wilderness. They were often behind the scenes and given no credit. Historian Keith Melder summed up the attitude of the era: "Woman should be naturally subordinate to man, yet her economic function was valued and her mind respected."[279] Of course, women could not be church leaders, for that would upset the ordering of society so carefully imposed in the law and in every institution, but ministers did encourage women to form supportive groups in the church and community.

In Vermont, historians Faith Pepe of Brattleboro and Constance M. McGovern urged researchers to look for a broader narrative of the socioeconomic status of women. Their work in the 1970s and 1980s was followed by Deborah Clifford's articles on suffrage and temperance and Lyn Blackwell's research on women in the nineteenth century. Their work was important to the historians who established the Vermont Women's History Project, an online reference for biographies of Vermont women, with essays on the narrative of women's work and life in Vermont. This rich history was mined from diaries, letters and materials in the archives of the state's historical society, as well as from town historical societies.

THE LIBERATION OF RELIGION:
MOTHER ANN LEE OF THE SHAKERS

Vermont women were often without wide contacts in the early days of settlement, but in the 1840s and 1850s, they could at least read literature and newspapers and thus become aware of a radical religion in which women were equal to men. Looking at the Enfield Shaker Village of Enfield, New Hampshire, on the border of Vermont, the picture broadens to include a woman who founded a religion and took on the mantle of "the female Christ."[280] Mother Ann Lee's religion attracted two hundred men and women from Vermont, and by 1850, 35 percent of the Enfield Shakers had come over from Vermont. Mother Ann Lee was one of the first women in America to lead a religious sect. Thus her story and religious influence is important in the study of women in northern New England and upstate New York.

Mother Ann Lee began life in 1736 in Manchester, England, and had entered the mills there to work by age eight. Cutting velvet, preparing cotton for looms or shearing fur on hats, her life consisted of working twelve hours a day and never attending school. She was illiterate but could memorize large sections of the Bible. In England, she became a "shaking Quaker," shouting, shaking and dancing to show inner feelings since she was part of a new group of believers.[281] Her sect believed that Christ was coming again to the world and would appear as a woman. She married at age twenty-six to a blacksmith and gave birth to four children. Unfortunately, they died, three as babies and one at age six. She then had a nervous breakdown and became sure that sex and marriage "were the root of all evil."[282] She concluded that "only a total denial of the body could purify her tortured soul."[283]

Ann Lee was a threat to the established Church of England, which she accused of being indifferent to the needs of the poor and promoting marriage. Her loud and feverish meetings led to "charges of fanaticism and heresy."[284] She had announced that she was married to Jesus Christ and that she had "walked, hand and hand, with him in heaven."[285] The result of this public declaration was that she was jailed and punished with a stoning. Yet nothing stopped her from formulating her religious beliefs. She could see that the New World would be a better place to obtain converts and spread her gospel. She and her followers landed in New York City in 1774, but when the American Revolution began, they left since they were peaceful and wanted to "withdraw from the world into a community of their own."[286] They traveled to a Native American area near Albany, New York, in 1776. Luckily, Lee developed good relations with the local natives, the Mahicans, who showed her community how to survive on local foods and medicines.

Once established, the Shakers could offer a way of life away from the material world and where they must "shun all sex, and confess all sins."[287] Followers should share their worldly goods, and thus deny self, but be at one with God since they were "devout socialists."[288] Thrift was sacred, and Lee dressed only in homespun articles, with a belief of "plainness in all things."[289] She wanted her followers to be stewards of the earth. Manual labor was sacred; cleanliness and order were high tenets. Obviously, a subset of her beliefs was freedom for women, and she strongly believed that her religion freed women "from oppression."[290] Also, women were to "complete the image of God."[291] Women were equal to men and could preach and speak up at meetings. Yet separation of the sexes was the rule in the community.

During the American Revolution, Lee was jailed with some of her followers in New York State since rebels thought she must have been a spy. Luckily, the governor released her due to respect for freedom of religion. She was one of the first in American history to speak out for conscientious objection to all wars. Ann Lee traveled for more than two years throughout Connecticut and Massachusetts as a missionary and was often beaten and castigated. Yet new communities of her followers were formed.

Her missionary travels had beaten the stuffing out of her. She sang and rocked in a primitive chair in her last weeks, and she died in 1784 at age forty-eight. The New Hampshire communities that attracted Vermonters formed after her death.

One of Mother Ann Lee's followers was Jane Elizabeth Snow Blanchard. She was born in Norwich, Vermont, in 1825 to a family of "meager means."[292] Hired out at age nine, she was overworked and returned to her family at age sixteen. While at home, she saw visions and heard voices. Learning about the Shakers, she walked the twenty-five miles to Enfield. She wanted "salvation to my sin sick soul."[293] Even though her family begged her to return, she rejected their entreaties and stayed until her death. She is an example of a Vermont woman who left an established farm life for what she believed would be a liberating religious community. She and others like her were rebelling against the norms and family patriarchy.

Race or prior religion did not preclude joining the Shakers. The highest membership was reached in 1845 with six thousand owning 100,000 acres of land. Their hard work, especially in the cultivation of herbs, fruits and flowers, was recognized far and wide. They were the first to dry seeds for packets, cut nails and metal pens, make a four-wheel dump wagon, vent beehives, make water-repellent fabric, weave palm leaf bonnets on a loom, market herb medicines and market manuals for the gardener. Their labor-saving inventions included a flat broom, a clothespin, a washing machine, a circular saw, an automatic spring, a turbine water wheel, a threshing machine, a tongue-and-groove machine, a revolving oven, an apple parer, a bread cutter, an herb presser, a pea sheller, a potato peeler, a peanut sheller and a static electricity generator. About forty inventions in total sprang from the sect's industrious workers.

Shaker Jane Blanchard of Norwich, Vermont. *Courtesy of the Canterbury Shaker Village Archives, Canterbury, New Hampshire.*

The Catholic mystic Thomas Merton summed up the Shaker gift to history as this: "The Shakers remain as witnesses to the fact that only humility keeps a man in communion with truth, and first of all with his own inner-truth."[294] He should have added that all of this was begun and led by a woman. Shakers continued for a while, with communities in Maine, Ohio, Kentucky and Indiana, twenty-four in all. Lower Shaker Village in Enfield, New Hampshire, was started in 1793 and ended in 1923. It is presently the location of a museum.

ACHSA SPRAGUE

Another leader with quite a following was Achsa Sprague of Plymouth, Vermont. Whenever she appeared to speak in the lecture halls or churches in the towns and cities of the fifteen Union states in the 1850s, it was standing room only. With her newspaper columns advocating for equal rights for women and prison reform, she was well known. Yet her talent as a trance lecturer, where she communed with the souls of her dead neighbors, transfixed her audiences. She was a medium who claimed to deliver messages from the spirit world to lift her listeners to new heights of awareness. Similar to Ann Lee, she "thought herself under the control of divine and mystic energies."[295]

Sprague was born in Plymouth in 1827, the sixth child in a family ruled by an alcoholic father. She attended her town's one-room schoolhouse and did so well that she eventually taught her classmates. It is not surprising that she became a teacher at the age of twelve, like many other young ladies of the era. Evidently, she taught until age twenty, when she had an attack of rheumatoid arthritis that confined her to her house for seven years, and she tried to function in a "partially crippled condition" for another six years.[296] "Angelic powers" transformed her in 1854 so that she could begin her mission as a trance medium and lecturer.[297] Her first public lecture was in South Reading on July 16, 1854. She was largely self-educated through her readings but did correspond with newspaper publisher Wendell Phillips, Ferrisburgh abolitionist Rowland Robinson and poet Henry W. Longfellow.

Sprague's diary detailed her life as an invalid; she studied nonreligious cures and then became an expert. Nothing worked, but she did not despair. When she could not walk, she rode a horse. Sprague credited the spirits with her recovery, and they called her to look at "divinity in nature."[298] Then, for six years, she toured the country as a "trance lecturer," giving her great fame and making her an important thinker on "spiritual and social truth."[299]

Sprague was an effective advocate of spiritualism, and this movement allowed women to speak before both genders. Since she was filling halls in Boston, she was urged to travel to Michigan, Baltimore, Philadelphia and the Midwest. In 1860, she received eighty-eight requests to speak. Men were especially moved. "The independent woman in the guise of the trance speaker enthralled her male audience."[300] She was willing to be looked at and willing to dress in a more flamboyant manner than the wives of men in the audiences. After

Achsa Sprague, spiritualist from Plymouth, Vermont. *Courtesy of the Vermont Historical Society.*

all, she was unconscious. Five men wrote to Sprague proposing marriage, even without having met her. Sprague wanted to remain single and loved her cause more than any one person. She was "very intelligent, sensitive and articulate."[301] Her publisher wrote that "her speaking was an inspiration. She possessed that power of the true orator—uplifting those she addressed into higher regions of thought and feeling."[302] People in Vermont came from miles away to hear and see "the preaching woman."[303]

Women had a role model and a "source of support in their own pursuit of independence."[304] Yet money was not her goal; as she stated, she wanted to impart truth and do good. The spirits called her to be "a teacher and a priestess divinely ordained."[305] However, she did earn enough money to support her parents and saved some $300 dollars. In addition, she frequently gave lectures to raise money for the poor.

She took up the cause of inmates of prisons, even addressing them at Providence, Rhode Island, and Philadelphia, Pennsylvania. In Boston, she visited the Charlestown State Prison and insisted on meeting with female prisoners. She was one of the first to blame the "social scheme" and the evils of liquor, not the criminals, for their situations.[306] She wrote poetry to denounce slavery and pleaded for emancipation of slaves long before the Civil War.

Sprague died at age thirty-four in 1862. The *Banner* published some of her poems, with a second edition shortly thereafter. She put Plymouth, Vermont, on the map for the spiritualists who gathered there many times up to 1875. Other mediums still quoted her, and her gravestone in the Plymouth cemetery has the words "I still live" engraved on it.

Indeed, her work did not end with her death. The Vermont Liberal Institute was created by friends of Sprague's in Plymouth, with the goal of educating young people. One graduate was John G. Sargent, a friend of President Calvin Coolidge (later becoming his attorney general), and Carrie Brown Coolidge, Coolidge's stepmother. It was a "community of learning" without requiring specific spiritual beliefs.[307] Students could be assured that they would be admitted to any New England college after this rigorous course of study.

EQUAL EDUCATION FOR WOMEN

A contemporary of Sprague's was Emma Hart Willard, who lived across the state in Middlebury, where she was advocating college-level education for women and writing textbooks in American history and astronomy.

Emma Willard, educator of Middlebury, Vermont. *Courtesy of the Middlebury College Archives.*

Born in Connecticut as one of seventeen children, she began teaching in Massachusetts but moved to Middlebury in 1807, where she met and married John Willard. Middlebury was already a "prosperous, highly cultured community with a fascinating social life."[308] It was a manufacturing center, becoming one of the fastest-growing towns in the state.

Willard opened a school in their home in 1814 for females to board and learn scientific and classical subjects at a higher level, similar to what they taught at nearby Middlebury College. Thus she was the first woman in the country to teach science and math to women. Yet she wanted different goals for women. She declared that instructions for women would be "first, moral and religious; second, literary; third, domestic; and fourth ornamental."[309] She justified the need for education for women who would mainly become mothers, not movers and shakers. Mothers could bring up better sons if they had an education themselves, and she felt that women were the superior teachers since it was in their "nature" to do so.[310] She wrote a pamphlet in 1819 to explain her philosophy called *A Plan for Improving Female Education*, with the goal of raising public monies for this purpose.[311]

Willard "was regal in appearance—a beautiful woman with classic features, gowned always in ribbed black silk or satin with a white mull turban on her head."[312] "She was a statuesque woman of 'classical features'—a Roman nose gave her a particularly strong profile."[313] Students characterized her as "a splendid looking woman...fully realized my idea of a queen."[314]

Her school in Middlebury was growing and thriving, but she must have known that Vermont was rather conservative and thus was anxious to find a more enlightened area and state. Her proposal to have a female seminary in Vermont did not get support. So, in 1819, a believer in her efforts convinced Governor DeWitt Clinton of New York to read her proposal, and he urged the legislature to support her desire to have a school for women. However, the men in the legislature refused, citing "concerns that education would harm women's health, create intellectual competition between the sexes, and disturb the social order."[315]

With Emma Willard's move to Troy, New York, and the opening of the Troy Female Seminary, which she ran from 1821 to 1838, she educated hundreds of women. She was the first woman to create a school of higher education for women and was successful without public funding. By 1872, twelve thousand had passed through the doors of her school, and their alumnae groups created "a women's network that stretched from New England to the deep south."[316] Her reach was great because in many cases she taught teachers who went on to form their own female academies. She trained more than two hundred teachers. Her former students created schools in South America and Greece. One of her students was Elizabeth Cady Stanton who, with Susan B. Anthony, fought for suffrage in America. Willard's school is still going strong as Emma Willard School.

ABBY MARIA HEMENWAY, STATE HISTORIAN

Born in 1828 in Ludlow and educated at Black River Academy, Abby Hemenway was a teacher and writer of poetry. In 1858, she collected poetry from state poets to publish *Poets and Poetry of Vermont* and from there decided to collect material for each town. This work, entitled *The Vermont Historical Gazetteer*, has been invaluable for historians and others who want to know the history of Vermont. She published a few town histories on her own and then turned to the state legislature for some minor funds. She was brave to take on this rather thankless project. In most towns, the resident historians were men. "No one else in the whole country attempted to do what Hemenway did, single-handedly collecting and publishing the history of every

Abby Hemenway, publisher and collector of town and village history, 1867–90. *Courtesy of the Vermont Historical Society.*

community in her state."[317] She had encouraged hundreds of volunteers to write of their churches, local businesses and their schools. It was not easy—she even had eleven lawsuits to contend with.

Historian Deborah Clifford summed up the legacy of Hemenway: "Her high purpose was to unite her fellow Vermonters through their shared recollections of the past, to give them a pride in their town and state, and in themselves as a people. As we would say today, she was seeking to enshrine a cultural memory."[318] This was a time when the early settlers were passing away from memory as well. Her collecting of history was a real first and was the forerunner of the Vermont Historical Society and all historical societies in the state. She also made a point of collecting women's stories and including social history when this was unusual for the time period.

NINETEENTH-CENTURY DAILY LIFE IN VERMONT FOR WOMEN: A CASE STUDY IN PEACHAM

It is rare that historians can accumulate enough material to describe a Vermont family through the eyes of women, but Lynn Bonfield and Mary Morrison have done that with *Roxana's Children: The Biography of a Nineteenth-Century Vermont Family*. They describe the family of Roxana Brown Walbridge Watts, who with her family saved three hundred family letters, thirty journals and diaries, photographs and artifacts so that a relative, Mary Morrison, and an archivist, Lynn Bonfield, could write an interesting book on women's lives in Vermont. The communications were often about health, the weather, crops, births, marriages, deaths, daily routine, annual events and local disasters. Some issues mentioned were national ones: the Civil War, the settling of the Midwest, the quest for education for women, the building of the railroad across the country and the rush for California gold.

Roxana, born in 1802, never traveled more than one hundred miles from her home in Peacham, in the Northeast Kingdom of Vermont. She married twice, to Daniel Walbridge in 1821 and to Lyman Watts in 1840 after the death of Daniel. She raised twelve children—nine of her own, two stepchildren and a grandson—with all twelve surviving childhood. She also made sure that her children were educated.

Roxana's parents were part of a group of six families from Charlestown, Massachusetts, who traveled to Vermont looking for cheap, fertile land in 1801. They arrived at Peacham to join 875 people in six miles square with a grammar school and a Congregational church already in the community. Roxana went to the local school and at age nineteen married Daniel Walbridge and moved to his farm of one hundred acres in Wolcott. They had five children, and she was expecting her sixth when Daniel died of "bilious complaint." She had to return to her parents' farm since her older children were girls. Without boys, she had no laborers.

Five years later, she married a widower, Lyman Watts, and went to live with him and his two boys. This was a marriage of convenience, but she was pleased to keep her children with her. Occasionally in these times, mothers would give up their children to families with more resources to raise them. Watts's farm consisted of sixty acres, with two oxen, two horses, one colt, eight cows, two heifers (young female caves) and forty sheep. He was a selectman and eventually became a state representative for Peacham. She proceeded to have three more children with him, giving birth to the last one at age forty-five. She wrote, "It seems to me some like living my life over again to be taking care of the little children again."[319] When her father died, her mother moved in to live with them for eighteen years.

Illness was a constant fear. Women often died in childbirth or from childbed infections. Roxana observed in 1843 that one in ten of the women giving

Grandmother and granddaughter, spinning wool. *Courtesy of the Vermont Historical Society.*

Sarah Walbridge Way, a daughter of Roxana Brown, in 1845. She worked in a Peacham weave shop and, in 1848, at textile mills in Lowell, Massachusetts. *Courtesy of Lynn A. Bonfield.*

birth had died in their town. Even Roxana's oldest daughter, Martha, died in childbirth in 1846.

Roxana's duties included cooking and baking on a wood stove (better than an open-hearth fireplace), making butter and cheese, dipping candles, cleaning, spinning yarn, weaving flannel and wool, knitting socks and washing. Mending was a relaxation. She also directed her children who worked with her. She found social life at the church to be enjoyable.

Five children of Roxana's went west; this was typical of the migration out of Vermont at this time in the 1830s. Farmers had begun to specialize, and some bought more and more land and were successful. Others who sold their land began to look to the West for adventure and a fresh start on flatter land. The transportation system in Vermont was primitive, with Boston markets very far away. According to Bonfield and Morrison, "the men experienced more gain than loss" with the move West.[320] "They found a longer growing season, cheap fertile soil, more forests to hunt game and farming like home…The women experienced more loss than gain."[321] They had homemaking without amenities, log cabins or worse, and "raising children in a rough country…By 1850, half of those born in Vermont lived outside the state."[322] Farmers, ministers, missionaries, soldiers and schoolteachers often left. Teaching could lead to a career in law or medicine. Craftsmen such as "carpenters, blacksmiths, shoemakers, printers, masons, coopers, and wheelwrights" found new opportunities in the Midwest.[323] Some returned, missing their tight-knit communities.

Sally Walbridge, the third child of the first marriage, in her teen years helped out a relative with childcare but wanted the freedom to work in a factory. Two other sisters were teachers. Small factories were started along rivers, and Sally worked at a local one but then left for Lowell and the larger factories. "The Merrimack River in Massachusetts was becoming the largest manufacturing center in the United States."[324] Owners set up boardinghouses with mandatory church attendance. The hours totaled seventy-three per week: thirteen per day Monday to Friday and eight on Saturday. Yet some women felt liberated being away from rural life with farm work. They earned cash, nine to thirteen dollars per month. Sally was there about a year during 1848–49 and then returned home to marry. Marriage and the end of factory work was expected of the mill girls and their families. Other Peacham girls had gone with Sally with the same expectations. After all, their other options, such as teaching, sewing and domestic work, paid much less. "Most factory girls, including Sally, experienced a new kind of power which came with a salary they could spend at their own discretion."[325]

EMPLOYMENT OUTSIDE THE HOME: TEXTILE MILLS

Another young New Englander, Mary Stiles Paul, left domestic work in Bridgewater, Vermont, to head to mill work in Lowell, Massachusetts. She wrote to her father in 1845:

I received your letter Thursday the 14th with much pleasure. I am well which is one comfort. My life and health are spared while others are cut off. Last Thursday one girl fell down and broke her neck which caused instant death. She was going in or coming out of the mill and slipped down it being very icy. The same day a man was killed by the [railroad] cars. Another had nearly all of his ribs broken. Another was nearly killed by falling down and having a bale of cotton fall on him. Last Tuesday we were paid. In all I had six dollars and sixty cents paid $4.68 for board. With the rest I got me a pair of rubbers and a pair of 50 .cts shoes. Next payment I am to have a dollar a week beside my board. We have not had much snow the deepest being not more than 4 inches. It has been very warm for winter…I can doff as fast as any girl in our room. I think I shall have frames before long…I think that the factory is the best place for me and if any girl wants employment I advise them to come to Lowell.

This from Mary S. Paul[326]

Yet new mills such as those in Lawrence, Massachusetts, were slums from the start. Conditions deteriorated. Processes were speeded up, and some women had to run four looms by themselves. And as a girl produced

Lowell Offering newspaper, a company-sponsored collection of writings by the female mill operatives. *Courtesy of the Lowell National Historical Park.*

more, the piece rate went down. When the prices declined, wages were cut. In the 1840s, the overseers were rewarded for getting the most work out of the girls. However, much earlier, in 1828 in Dover, New Hampshire, four hundred women walked off the job protesting fines for lateness. This was the first strike for women and second for factory workers (the first was by children in Paterson, New Jersey). In the 1830s, there were sporadic walkouts. In 1836, with a wage cut, 1,500 Lowell women workers marched through town singing:

Oh isn't it a pity, such a pretty girl as I
Should be sent into a factory to pine away and die
Oh I cannot be a slave

Oh I will not be a slave
For I'm so fond of liberty
I cannot be a slave.[327]

Owners starved them into submission and threw them out of their boardinghouses. Yet the girls held out for a month while leaders were fired and blacklisted. Some women started writing protest materials, but not in the company newspaper. They formed the Female Labor Reform Association in 1845. They joined with male workers in other Massachusetts factories and even petitioned the state legislature for a ten-hour day. Their petitions were ignored. By the late 1840s, no one believed that factory work was a blessing, but millions of new immigrants were arriving. The Irish would take the jobs. In 1845, the mill girls were 90 percent native; by 1850, 50 percent were Irish immigrants. The Vermonters went home.

But change was coming. There was abolitionism, prohibition and suffrage to elevate women into political actors and advocates.

Abolition

Female antislavery movements threatened the establishment more than other groups because they "participated in the political process by circulating petitions among women, appealing for state and federal legislation to abolish slavery in the District of Columbia, eliminate the interstate slave trade, or otherwise undermine the legal status of slavery."[328] Many Vermont women felt a certain female solidarity with the female slaves. The Quaker women strongly advocated not buying anything made by slaves, and there is evidence of that at Rokeby in Ferrisburgh. Vermont women had to make more products themselves. For instance, they would use maple sugar instead of sugar since slave labor was involved in harvesting the sugar plant. Their clothes would be homespun rather than made from cotton.

Many historical societies in Vermont have preserved documents from meetings of their female abolition societies. There were societies in Bellingham, Norwich, Weybridge, Waitsfield, Cornwall and Randolph. In 1835, 420 women signed an antislavery petition in Starksboro to send to Congress.

Minutes from the Norwich Female Abolition Society commence in 1843 with a goal "to use all means sanctioned by law, humanity, and religion, for the entire and unconditional abolition of slavery in this country, for the elevation of the character and condition of people of color, and their admission to equal rights and privileges with the whites."[329] Women packed up boxes of clothing for slaves to use once they reached Canada. They also began cent societies with the purpose of raising funds for projects. In Norwich, the Female Cent Society was organized in 1859 as an auxiliary to the Vermont Domestic Missionary Society. Women were to pay one cent per week or fifty-two cents per year to help pay for assistance to escaped slaves.[330] This was part of the dissension building up to the Civil War, but it should not be forgotten that women involved in this movement became political actors, writing constitutions, voting for their own officers, organizing meetings, fundraising and plotting ways to end slavery. They were becoming political actors in their towns and on the state level.

CIVIL WAR SUPPORT

Female patriots supported the soldiers during the Civil War. Soldiers' aid societies were organized in towns to help with relief as part of the United States Sanitary Commission. Members sent flannel drawers, stockings, flannel shirts, pillowcases, handkerchiefs, slippers, dry apples, chestnuts, currants and even cakes of soap.

Yet the women knew as the men went off to war that they would be running the farms back home with elderly men or male children as their helpers. As Vermont Civil War historian Howard Coffin wrote, the "hardships of the wartime home front fell on the women."[331] Women had to learn to run a farm or manage a shop. At the end of the war, widows often tried to find the remains of their dead husbands and reinter them in

Charles C. and Mary Staples of Williamstown. He enlisted in Company E, Eighth Vermont Infantry Regiment, in 1861 and was mustered out in 1865. *Courtesy of Paul G. Zeller and the Williamstown Historical Society.*

Daniel C. and Celia Townsend. He enlisted in Company D, Twelfth Vermont Infantry Regiment, in 1862 and was discharged in 1863 after contracting typhoid fever. *Courtesy of Paul G. Zeller and the Williamstown Historical Society.*

Vermont cemeteries or put up memorial stones. One widow, Frances Bixby, arranged for her husband's memorial stone in Chelsea, as he had been buried at Andersonville, the horrible Confederate prison. She wrote this epitaph for his gravestone: "God has marked every sorrowing day, And numbered every secret tear."[332]

Prohibition

The prohibition of alcohol was an effort by women and some men, mainly ministers, to reform men. If fathers did not drink away their wages, it was reasoned, they could bring more money home to their wives and children. In 1875, women in Burlington organized the Vermont Women's Christian Temperance Society, and many chapters in Vermont organized and lobbied for the first state temperance education law in 1882. There had been a state prohibition law since 1852, but that did not stop the liquor from flowing and the saloons being filled with male customers. Burlington, Rutland and St. Albans did not enforce prohibition, with the result being more crime and disorder.

The temperance women of St. Albans planned to enlist the sympathies of the town leaders, get pledges from property holders that their buildings would not be leased for drinking and form a committee to go from home to home and to liquor dealers to obtain personal pledges. One day, fifty members sang and marched through the streets of St. Albans, extracting

Norwich Fidelis Bible class, Norwich Congregational Church; early twentieth-century meetings would change women. *Courtesy of the Norwich Historical Society.*

The Drunkard's Wife, a painting by Thomas Waterman Wood depicting an accusing spouse imploring a saloonkeeper in Montpelier to help her stop her husband's drinking. *Courtesy of the T.W. Wood Gallery.*

promises of temperance from hotel owners and saloon bartenders. They may have not closed many saloons, but this was a "baptism of power and liberty" for American women.[333]

Women stated that they were guarding their homes and the homes of their sisters. Vermont women were part of the national convention of the Woman's Christian Temperance Union, which men were not allowed to join. They created a state WCTU in Montpelier in 1875 made up of many churchwomen who wanted each village to have a chapter and even children's temperance societies. Middle-class women, now with more time since the invention of the sewing machine and cook stoves, wanted a place to befriend other women and give voice to their own talents and abilities. Women obtained the vote in school matters in their towns so that they could gain access to schools and place temperance textbooks in the hands of youngsters. A good example would be this 1844 temperance circular in Chittenden County:

To the Freemen of Chittenden County:

The use of ardent spirits is pregnant with iniquity and crime. Abolish their use, and you almost abolish our criminal code, for 9/10's of our criminals, date their fall from virtue to infamy, at the time when they first put the rum glass to their lips. From the fashionable potation at the splendid bar, the drunkard gradually descends to the three cent grog shop, where he commits the deed, which either consigns him to the walls of the state's prison or a murderer's grave. The strongest advocates of the practice dare not assert that men are made more moral or more upright by drunkenness. Shall we then in vain implore the aide of the moralist or the Christian? We spend more on liquor here than on flour.

The Norwich water fountain was provided by the Norwich chapter of the Woman's Christian Temperance Union, with the goal of providing cool drinking water that would stop people from drinking alcoholic beverages. The bronze plaque noted, "Water is Life." *Courtesy of the Norwich Historical Society.*

In view of these stubborn facts, will not every person who has an interest in the public morals and private property, refuse to sustain or support men, who foster and cherish this degrading, devouring and demoralizing evil?[334]

The WCTU members were "disciples of Christ."[335] The women prayed and sang hymns. Prohibition was the main goal, but there was also a drive for kindergartens, prison reform, child labor laws, laws to protect working women and the vote. The rationale was that these goals would improve life for a mother and a wife. This was the popular advocacy group for women in America.

Suffrage

After women became involved in the abolition and temperance movements, they began to ask for their political rights. When advocating for an end to slavery and an end to liquor, women had to employ men to enact change.

Lucy Stone, one of the earliest lecturers for women's rights, spoke to Vermont audiences. *Courtesy of the Library of Congress.*

They could not vote these measures and reforms into action by themselves. One of the most famous orators of the day and a prominent abolitionist, Lucy Stone, traveled through Vermont lecturing along the way, and some Vermonters went to national conventions. When challenged that the women's rights movement was just a few frustrated women, Lucy countered with these words in 1855:

The last speaker alluded to this movement as being that of a few disappointed women. From the first years of which my memory stretches I have been a disappointed woman. When, with my brother, I reached forth after sources of knowledge, I was reproved with, "It isn't fit for you; it doesn't belong to women." Then there was but one college in the world where women were admitted and that was in Brazil, I would have found my way there, but by the time I was prepared to go one was opened in the young state of Ohio—the first in the U.S where negroes and women could enjoy opportunities with white men. I was disappointed when I came to seek a profession…every employment was closed to me, except those of the teacher, the seamstress and the housekeeper.

In education, in marriage, in religion, in everything, disappointment is the lot of woman. It shall be the business of my life to deepen this disappointment in every woman's heart until she bows down to it no longer. I wish that women, instead of begging of their fathers and brothers the latest and gayest new bonnet, would ask of them their rights.[336]

Lucy, her husband (Henry Blackwell) and Julia Ward Howe, composer of the "Battle Hymn of the Republic" and head of the New England Women's Suffrage Association, traveled through Vermont many times.

CLARINA HOWARD NICHOLS

In Vermont, Clarina Howard Nichols of Townshend was the first well-known female leader for reform on women's issues. She grew up in West Townshend, and her family raised her to be an excellent housekeeper and frugal housewife. Her mistreatment by her first husband and father of her children began her long journey into reform. When she wanted a divorce without losing custody of her children, she came up against the existing legal system.

She was the first woman to speak before the Vermont legislature, in 1852, and was editor of the newspaper, the *Windham County Democrat*. She wanted women to vote in school meetings. She wore bloomers on the streets of Brattleboro, and she articulated the reasons why women should have the vote. Speaking before the national convention in New York City in 1853, she implored that "she may have a due control over her own moral, intellectual, and social interests...I am deprived of the power of protecting myself and my children, because I do not possess the power which ought to belong to me as a mother."[337] She was "gentle but firm. She was blessed with an even buoyant temperament and a keen sense of humor. She was able to seize the essential points of an argument and develop them clearly and incisively."[338]

Nichols joined the suffrage lecture circuit with Lucy Stone and Susan B. Anthony. In 1855, she moved to Kansas and helped write that state's constitution. She wanted to tackle a new state and set up new laws. Vermont was just too conservative, with patriarchy too entrenched. But in Vermont she got the courage to speak about her convictions.

ANNETTE PARMELEE: THE SUFFRAGE HORNET

Vermont's suffrage association was largely led by Annette Parmelee. She pushed for the vote in municipal elections, which was obtained in 1917 for tax-paying women. She presented many arguments in support of the vote for women. Speaking in Randolph in 1917, she said, "Woman is fast emerging from ignorance into knowledge, from slavery to near freedom, from impotence to power, due to Christianity and education."[339] She explained that women could now be lawyers, doctors and managers of hospitals. Yet she focused on the home, where there should be equal power—"equal rights mean equal responsibility, equal justice to working men and women, equal pay for women who do work equal to that of men."[340] She also led a drive to have Vermont become the thirty-sixth state to ratify the Nineteenth Amendment, giving women the vote. Governor Clement would not call a special session to do that, and in 1919, he vetoed suffrage for women. Vermont women had to wait for the Susan B. Anthony amendment to the Constitution, which was ratified by Tennessee and thus became law in 1920.

Immigration

The unskilled and the skilled were coming to Vermont from Scotland, Ireland, Italy, Sweden, Wales and other European countries. The second half of the nineteenth century saw an influx of workers, who provided labor for the marble and slate industries. French Canadian families came to Vermont textile mills, and whole families were put to work. So many children were involved that child labor conditions were investigated by the National Child Labor Committee and new laws were created.

In Rutland during the 1850s and 1860s, large Irish families lived in tenements. Women would tend gardens to grow their vegetables and often had a cow, a few pigs and chickens. Anything else would be bought at the company store at inflated prices. Men were away at the quarry or mill, so household work was done by women. Wood was the heating and cooking source, so air pollution added to the railroad steam pollution. Poor sanitation added to the illnesses.

The Vermont Marble Company did address health needs in the community by hiring the first industrial nurse in the 1890s, Ada Mayo Stewart, and by building a local hospital for workers and families to receive free treatment.

The 1907 visit by anarchist Emma Goldman, reported in her autobiography, presented Barre, Vermont, as a city of corruption, drinking and prostitution. The police sent her on her way before her last meeting after a two-week stay. She was too close to disclosing the behavior of the mayor and chief of police.

Barre, with its Socialist Labor Hall, was famous in Vermont, especially when the children of the Lawrence, Massachusetts strikers were brought into homes to be fed and clothed during the labor strike of 1912. This exodus of children "attracted enormous sympathy for the strikers' cause."[341] Textile workers in Lawrence, mainly women and children, had gone on strike due to wage cuts. They organized a moving picket line and waved signs—"We

"Anemic Little Spinner in North Pownal Cotton Mill, 1910." Photograph by Lewis Hine and symbol of child labor in Vermont. French Canadian families immigrated to Vermont, where the whole family worked and children often missed school. *Courtesy of the Library of Congress.*

Want Bread, but We Want Roses, Too"—so the strike is known as the Bread and Roses Strike, led by the Industrial Workers of the World.

Margaret Sanger, a nurse helping the children, described them as without underwear and with coats shredded and torn. The future birth control advocate questioned how the children could endure the winter weather in

Socialist Labor Hall of Barre, with children of strikers from Lawrence, Massachusetts, 1912. *Courtesy of Aldrich Library Collection, Barre, Vermont.*

such rags. Thirty-five children were sent to the Italian families in Barre. The Labor Hall was a gathering spot for dances and a co-op. It was also an end point for these children before they were taken in by local families.

Union meetings were held in the labor hall from 1900 to 1936. Unions were needed, with sixty-eight granite quarries offering workers low wages with tough conditions. The socialist labor movement had important goals, one of which was equal civil and political rights for all men and women.

EDNA BEARD AND CONSUELO BAILEY, POLITICAL FIRSTS FOR WOMEN

With women finally gaining seats in the House and Senate in Vermont, much of the legislation between 1920 and 1940 focused on protecting women, children and minors. Edna Beard was the first woman elected to the Vermont legislature, in 1920, and her first bill was designed to help gain funds for mothers whose husbands were incapacitated. In 1923, she was the first woman elected to the Vermont Senate, and her first bill there made it legal for sheriffs to hire female deputies. She had been a teacher in the Orange schools and in 1906 had been elected the town school superintendent. She was the town treasurer and a mainstay at the Congregational church.

She won her race for the Vermont House because forty women registered to vote. She worked on an amendment to the Vermont Constitution to ensure the right to vote for women and to get Vermont to approve the suffrage amendment at the federal level. In 1922, she ran for and won a

Above: Teacher and town school superintendent Edna Beard and her students, 1906. *Courtesy of the Vermont Historical Society.*

Left: Edna Beard, the first woman to be elected to the Vermont House of Representatives, in 1920. She was also the first woman elected to the Vermont Senate, in 1923. *Courtesy of the Vermont Historical Society.*

seat as a state senator but did not run again due to ill health; she died of a heart attack in 1928.

She must have been an inspiration for Consuelo Northrup Bailey, who attended the University of Vermont, graduated in 1921 and attended Boston University's School of Law, where she was one of twenty-five women surrounded by one thousand men. She found a way up the ladder of law in Vermont, winning female firsts along the way. She was the first female city prosecutor for Burlington, the first woman elected state's attorney in 1926 and the first female lawyer to try a murder case. After marrying another lawyer, Henry A. Bailey, she was elected to the state legislature as a representative from 1950 to 1956, becoming the first female Speaker in 1953.

Consuelo Northrup Bailey, the first female lieutenant governor in the nation, in 1954. *Courtesy of the Vermont Historical Society.*

Bailey was the first female elected lieutenant governor in the country in 1954. As she recounted in her autobiography, during her campaign she was required to enter a milking contest in Randolph. Since she had been a farmer in her teens in Fairfield, she was not phased. As she recalled, "I had to win. Vermont farmers' wives would be delighted. There were votes in every splash into the pail."[342] Once elected, Bailey focused on public school construction, construction of the interstate highways and investment in the University of Vermont. With her husband's illness, she left state government but served as a national leader for the Republican Party.

DOROTHY THOMPSON AND GRACE COOLIDGE: TWO HUMANITARIANS

Two famous women had an impact on Vermont and the national stage, but each had rather obscure beginnings. Dorothy Thompson was born in Lancaster, New York, to a poor Methodist minister and his wife in 1893.

When other children came along, the funds were stretched very tight, and Dorothy's grandmother stepped in to prevent a fourth child. The potion she administered to her daughter was deadly. Dorothy, now motherless, then clashed with her father's second wife and was sent to live with two aunts in Chicago. That was where she finally had encouragement to go to a junior college and then transfer to Syracuse University.

In 1914, she began her career as a campaigner for suffrage in Buffalo, New York, and then took a ship to Europe to begin a career in journalism. She wrote in Vienna for the *Public Ledger* newspaper. When it merged with the *New York Evening Post*, she became the queen of the overseas press corps, the first woman to head a foreign news bureau. She impressed Europeans with her "brightness and charm."[343] As the playwright Carl Zuckmayer wrote of Thompson in her late twenties, "She was marvelously healthy; her face always looked as if she had just been running in a stiff sea or a mountain breeze…Even when her fine, well-proportioned figure was becoming a little

Dorothy Thompson visiting with Smith College students. A famous radio commentator from 1934 to 1946, she also a Vermont preservationist and advocate for farm life. *Courtesy of the Sophia Smith Collection, Smith College, Northampton, Massachusetts.*

plump, she loved to wear very light, rather girlish dresses…she took time to live, to be a woman and a human being."[344]

When Dorothy met the famous American writer Sinclair Lewis in Europe, they fell in love and left their respective spouses in 1927. With her subsequent marriage to Lewis, she became famous, and their honeymoon was covered by journalists the world over. However, the Vermont story began when Lewis bought the Connett place and adjacent Chase farm to create Twin Farms. This property of more than three hundred acres was in Barnard, Vermont, and became their summer retreat. There she began to care about the preservation of Vermont and farming. She had already had an impact on international and national affairs, speaking out against Hitler and his henchmen. From 1934 to 1946, she not only wrote a column for the *Herald Tribune* but was also a radio commentator and lecturer. In 1939, she was on the air for fifteen days describing the Hitler-led German invasions of Europe. She roused the American public and helped ready them to enter World War II.

She and former first lady Grace Coolidge both worked to rescue Jewish children in the years before war was declared by America. Grace Coolidge was a member of the Northampton Massachusetts Refugee Committee that, in 1939, offered homes for twenty-five Jewish children, those like Anne Frank who wanted to flee Nazi Germany. Grace was born in Burlington, Vermont, graduated from the University of Vermont and married Calvin Coolidge of Plymouth. He was the shy one; she was the extrovert. She remembered names and faces and was open and warm to those she met. She was well known in Northampton, where she taught deaf children before her marriage. When thirtieth U.S. president Coolidge died, she spent much time in Northampton, where they had raised their children. Her committee appealed to the U.S. State Department, and the request was folded into the Wagner Rogers Bill, which would have admitted twenty thousand German refugee children aged fourteen or younger. It failed to gain

Grace Coolidge, first lady from 1923 to 1929, was a member of the Northampton, Massachusetts Refugee Committee, in 1939, and a Vermont preservationist. *Courtesy of the Calvin Coolidge Memorial Foundation, Plymouth, Vermont.*

support, with only 26 percent of the public in favor—it was thought that the economic depression of the 1930s had left American children with needs that should be met first.

Dorothy Thompson rallied national support with her radio commentaries and newspaper columns. She even called for an international organization to coordinate all refugee migration. After Kristallnacht, she spoke out even more since she felt that non-Jews must "speak our sorrow and indignation and disgust in so many voices that they WILL be heard."[345]

Both Coolidge and Thompson were unsuccessful in trying to save children like Anne Frank, but they did their best, taking a stand that was rare, brave and unpopular. If they were listened to, thousands of children might have survived the Holocaust.

During World War II, Thompson tried to save Vermont farms by creating a Land Corps for farmers in the state. She had enjoyed farming in Barnard and wanted others to have the same experience as they came out of the cities for the summer. In 1942, she created a pilot program that brought six hundred high school–aged youths from cities to Vermont. She talked her friends, poet Robert Frost and writer Dorothy Canfield Fisher, into promoting the program and enlisted Governor William Wills and Lieutenant Governor Mortimer Proctor to praise these sunshine boys and girls over the state's radio stations. Thompson was so encouraged that she wanted to create a new women's land army next.

After the war, Thompson continued to champion unpopular causes and lost much of her support from newspaper publishers. Still, she was beloved in Barnard for her preservationist policies, buying farms for German refugees and saving Silver Lake. Her friends created a memorial park in her memory right next to the lake after her death.

Grace Coolidge thought that she should help Vermont preserve the village and birthplace of her husband in Plymouth. She gave Calvin Coolidge's homestead to the State of Vermont as it bought his birthplace. Her son, John, continued purchases of homes and land until the whole village was preserved.

PROGRESS FOR WOMEN

After thousands of hippies moved into Vermont and the legislature was reapportioned, changes were in the wind for women as well. Democratic governor Philip Hoff established the Governor's Commission on the Status of Women. In the 1970s, the legislature prohibited discrimination in hiring based on gender, and abortion was legalized. The Equal Rights Amendment was proposed after a committee was formed in 1985 to support the national amendment, which read, "Equality of rights under the law shall not be denied or abridged by the United States or by any State on account of sex." There was much opposition centering on abortion rights and gay rights. This meant that on November 4, 1986, the Vermont State ERA was defeated. There were still conservatives in the hills of Vermont.

Madeleine May Kunin and Esther Hartigan Sorrell, founder of the Vermont Democratic Party, ran campaigns to become representatives in the legislature in 1972 and won. Kunin was the mother of four children, ages eleven, nine, six and two. Her husband was an assistant professor of medicine at the University of Vermont. She called herself a homemaker but had written articles and taught for many years.

Kunin had been a very shy child who was transported in 1940 to America at age six when her mother decided that they had to leave Europe with the threat of Hitler. Madeleine played the role of the silent observer in her school years but was forced into speaking if she wanted a political life. She feared

Governor Madeleine Kunin. *Courtesy of the Vermont State Archives and Records Administration.*

speaking, worrying that her "articulated words would come out wrong, too angry, too passive, or be misunderstood."[346]

Yet finally having something to say, she was fueled by the idea of women in politics. She feared not being liked by what she said. However, as she moved along in politics, she learned that her answers did carry a price and yet the strength of her words was worth the price. After all, the vanguards were the outspoken feminists of the 1970s. They had cleared the way for her. She had an "informal, sincere manner, combined with knowledge of her subject" and was known for her "persistence, patience, tenacity, physical stamina, and grace."[347]

In 1985, she was elected the first female governor in Vermont. Kunin became the first woman to serve three terms as governor of any state and the fourth woman in the United States to be elected governor in her own right. She worked on children's services and doubled funding for public education. She established the Vermont Housing and Land Conservation Trust Fund to create affordable housing and land preservation. Governor Kunin promoted and encouraged as many women as possible from the corner office.

When she decided not to run again for governor, she was tapped by President Bill Clinton to be his deputy secretary of education and then his ambassador to Switzerland. In her retirement, she is presently writing a book on public policy and day care in America.

CONCLUSION

Early Native American women were involved in a "great range of women's economic, social, and religious roles."[348] This was barely understood by the Europeans who came to Vermont and conquered the territory. Native women had power and autonomy within their clans. Europeans just saw "wives… treated as slaves."[349] Molly Ockett was surely a powerful figure growing up as a native but also cooperating and assisting the settlers as much as she could, while keeping her independence.

With the settlement of Vermont after the end of the French and Indian War of 1763, settlers came into the area "hellbent for liberty at any cost," meaning that the constitution and the republic would balance freedom and unity.[350] Someone forgot to tell the women! The legal constraints of the colonies would follow the women who settled Vermont. They would be legally covered by their husbands. This meant that they would mainly be in their households and raise their children; their only public activities would be with their churches. Their main tasks would be to survive the frontier life. Yet female rebels in the state sought more for their sex and thought that equality with men should be a goal. Many were reformers focusing on abolition, temperance and suffrage. Once they found their public voice, they wanted their public vote so long denied until 1920.

Women slowly edged into politics, the first being Edna Beard. But the migration out of the state from 1840 to 1950 often took the best and the brightest. For example, Clarina Howard Nichols tried to bring reform to Vermont but gave up and went to Kansas. By 1850, 145,000 had left, and that was before the Civil War widened the horizons for many rural farm families to add to the exodus.

However, the repopulation of Vermont between 1960 and 1970 brought in new people with progressive ideas; some were hippies leaving behind the Vietnam War. This 14 percent jump in population came with intentions to "slow down, taste life, understand the planet, sink roots, and manage their own lives."[351] A new "humanistic, decentralist order" was possible, and women stepped up to participate.[352] The arc of Madeleine Kunin's career was such that she took advantage of new attitudes and brought women into the government to bring about this new type of order.

A recent look at women's participation in Vermont politics is promising. In the legislature, about 30 percent are women, making it one of the most progressive in the country. If one studies town meetings, 48 percent of the local participants in the leadership of the towns are women. Women are on the brink of leadership in the state of Vermont.

CONCLUSION

From the opening poem to the last sentence in this book, I have tried to give a voice to the voiceless. When possible, I have quoted from poems, sermons and speeches to show how articulate and thoughtful most of these people were. Their own voices merit inclusion in Vermont's state history. Since I teach Vermont history for the state's community college system, I am well aware of what should be taught in a survey course and the importance of covering topics in social, political and economic institutions. But also in our curriculum, students are asked to evaluate the significance of ethnic and minority groups in the state and to interpret the experience of Vermont women in different historical periods. Hopefully a more detailed history of these topics in these pages will be an important addition to this course of study.

As a teacher at the state's community college, I have observed that most of my students are women. With the inclusion of women in the historical narrative, they will find more people in history with whom to identify. If this book inspires one woman to change her perception of her own potential, it will have been worth the effort.

For those readers who have studied Vermont, I hope that this new material will enrich their view of the state. Inspired by Howard Zinn and his book, *A People's History of the United States*, I have tried to highlight "the past's fugitive moments of compassion" and not the victories from wars.[353] Yet I have not focused on victims, but rather on change agents. Those people who made a difference to their gender, their race or their family band have the most exciting and meaningful stories to tell. Hopefully, all of us will be the richer from the mining of these stories of hope, frustration and striving for excellence.

Notes

Introduction

1. Fisher, *Vermont Tradition*, 6.
2. Elise A. Guyette, "Vermont Women's Historiography" http://www.womenshistory.vermont.gpv/VTWomeninHistory/Historiography.
3. Ibid.
4. Ibid.
5. Evans, *Born for Liberty*, 3.

Part I

6. Jeannine Bunnell Smith, *Dawnland Voice* newsletter, Koasek Traditional Band of the Sovereign Abenaki Nation of Post Mills, Vermont, 2008.
7. Johnson, *Narrative of Mrs. Johnson*, 132.
8. Calloway, *Western Abenakis of Vermont*, 28.
9. Ibid., 31.
10. Johnson, *Narrative of Mrs. Johnson*, 140.
11. Calloway, *Western Abenakis of Vermont*, 33.
12. Sherman, Sessions and Potash, *Freedom and Unity*, 8.
13. Donnis, *History of Shelburne Farms*, 28.
14. Bearse, *Vermont*, 41.
15. Hanson, *America's First People*, v.
16. Ibid.

17. Mann, *1491*, 36.
18. Hanson, *America's First People*, 59.
19. Haviland and Power, *Original Vermonters*, 72.
20. Ibid., 151.
21. Mann, *1491*, 39.
22. Albers, *Hands on the Land*, 48.
23. Ibid., 68.
24. Daniels, *Vermont Indians*, 7.
25. Foster and Cowan, eds., *In Search of New England's Past*, 3.
26. Ibid., 142–43.
27. Ibid.
28. Ibid., 141.
29. Mann, *1491*, 44.
30. Ibid., 46.
31. Haviland and Power, *Original Vermonters*, 205.
32. Ibid., 209.
33. Albers, *Hands on the Land*, 63.
34. Haviland and Power, *Original Vermonters*, 207.
35. Albers, *Hands on the Land*, 70.
36. Ibid., 72.
37. Haviland and Power, *Original Vermonters*, 216.
38. Calloway, *First Peoples*, 185.
39. Haviland and Power, *Original Vermonters*, 214.
40. Calloway, *Western Abenakis of Vermont*, 160.
41. Ibid., 171.
42. Ibid., 116.
43. Johnson, *Narrative of Mrs. Johnson*, 8.
44. Ibid., 18.
45. Ibid., 49.
46. Ibid., 70.
47. Ibid., 71.
48. Ibid., 76–77.
49. Ulrich, *Good Wives*, 213.
50. Calloway, *Western Abenakis of Vermont*, 178.
51. Johnson, *Narrative of Mrs. Johnson*, 133.
52. Elnu Petition for Recognition, 2011.
53. Calloway, *Western Abenakis of Vermont*, 181.
54. Elnu Petition for Recognition, 2011.
55. Calloway, *Western Abenakis of Vermont*, 83.

56. Ibid., 85.
57. Ibid., 16.
58. Haviland and Power, *Original Vermonters*, 246.
59. Ibid., 247.
60. Albers, *Hands on the Land*, 69.
61. Calloway, *Western Abenakis of Vermont*, 183.
62. Ibid., 192.
63. Ibid., 193.
64. Ibid.
65. Ibid., 196.
66. Ibid., 202.
67. Ibid., 208.
68. Ibid., 210.
69. Ibid., 217.
70. Ibid., 223.
71. Johnson family papers, the Vermont Historical Society.
72. Calloway, *Western Abenakis of Vermont*, 225.
73. Swanton Historical Society website.
74. Calloway, *Western Abenakis of Vermont*, 230.
75. Ibid., 234.
76. Ibid., 237.
77. Ibid., 240.
78. Calloway, *Dawnland Encounters*, 244.
79. Calloway, *First Peoples*, 230.
80. Ibid., 233.
81. Calloway, *Indian History of an American Institution*, 74.
82. McBride, *Women of the Dawn*, 45.
83. Ibid., 46.
84. Ibid., xi.
85. Ibid., 48.
86. Ibid., 53.
87. Ibid., 53–54.
88. Ibid., 57.
89. Ibid., 55.
90. Grumet, *Northeastern Indian Lives*, 335.
91. McBride, *Women of the Dawn*, 63.
92. Ibid., 64.
93. Ibid., 62–63.
94. Ibid., 67.

95. Coffin, Curtis and Curtis, *Guns Over the Champlain Valley*, 49–53.

96. Apess, "Eulogy on King Philip," in *A Son of the Forest and Other Writings.*

97. Calloway, *First Peoples*, 132.

98. Ibid.

99. Calloway, *Western Abenakis of Vermont*, 248.

100. Calloway, *Indian History of an American Institution*, 155.

101. Wiseman, *Voice of the Dawn*, 114.

102. Ibid., 115.

103. Ibid., 138.

104. Ibid.

105. Coolidge, *The Autobiography of Calvin Coolidge*, 16.

106. Wiseman, *Voice of the Dawn*, 146.

107. Sherman, Sessions and Potash, *Freedom and Unity*, 429.

108. Gallagher, *Breeding Better Vermonters*, 32.

109. Sherman, Sessions and Potash, *Freedom and Unity*, 431.

110. Ibid., 430.

111. Ibid.

112. Ibid., 431.

113. Ibid., 83.

114. Wiseman, *Voice of the Dawn*, 146. Along with this movement in the United States, the theory of eugenics was developed in the 1850s in Europe, where concepts of scientific plant and animal breeding were applied to humans. Racial and ethnic superiority and inferiority would be measured, and with sterilization, the obvious "problem" races or immigrant groups would be candidates for no further propagation.

115. Jeanne Brink, presentation at Hartland Historical Society, May 2011.

116. Vermont Public Radio news, May 3, 2011.

117. Elnu Abenaki memo on Vermont legislature, January 20, 2011. In Jodi Picoult's novel *Second Glance*, published in 2003, she re-created the agony of an Abenaki woman facing eugenics and the destruction of her family. Picoult quoted from Perkins and his reports using material such as this: "The right of the individual cannot be fully safeguarded when he is being compelled to support in the midst of his community the lawless, the immoral, the degenerate, and the mentally defective." *Lessons from a Eugenical Survey of Vermont: First Annual Report* (1927).

118. Wiseman, *Voice of the Dawn*, 152.

119. Wiseman, *Reclaiming the Ancestors*, 13.

120. Ibid.

121. Calloway, *Western Abenakis of Vermont*, 249.

122. Wiseman, *Voice of the Dawn*, 183.

123. Ibid., 186.

124. Moody, "People of Color," 11.

125. Vermont Women's History Project website, Grandma Lampman.

126. Lampman-Larivee, Vermont Public Radio commentary, March 27, 2009.

127. Calloway, *Western Abenakis of Vermont*, 250.

128. Vermont Digger website, February 27, 2012.

129. Elnu memo, January 20, 2011.

Part II

130. Roth, *Democratic Dilemma*, 295.

131. Ibid.

132. Ibid.

133. Gerzina, *Mr. and Mrs. Prince*, 156.

134. Ibid., 186.

135. Ibid., 79.

136. Gerzina, VPR commentary, March 2010, http://www.vpr.net/episode/48135/gerzina-story-lucy-prince.

137. Brace, *Blind African Slave*.

138. Haynes, "The Battle of Lexington," in Bogin, *William and Mary Quarterly* 42 (third series), no. 4.

139. Haynes, *Nature and Importance of True Republicanism*.

140. Ibid.

141. Ibid.

142. Ibid.

143. Guyette, *Discovering Black Vermont*, 53.

144. Ibid., 54.

145. Ibid., 57.

146. Ibid., 54.

147. Lovejoy, "Life of Ichabod Twilight."

148. School materials, Old Stone House Museum, Brownington, Vermont.

149. Sermons, Old Stone House Museum; school materials, Old Stone House Museum.

150. Sermons, Old Stone House Museum; school materials, Old Stone House Museum.

151. Ibid.

152. Mosher, *Vermont Life* magazine, Autumn 1996. The University of Vermont credits Andrew Harris as the first African American to graduate from the University of Vermont in 1838. He was refused admission to Middlebury and Union College. The reasons for being denied admission are not clear.

153. Sherman, Sessions and Potash, *Freedom and Unity*, 188.

154. Roth, *Democratic Dilemma*, 12.

155. Sherman, Sessions and Potash, *Freedom and Unity*, 192.

156. Rokeby papers.

157. Irvine, "Martin H. Freeman of Rutland."

158. Ibid., 77.

159. Ibid.

160. Ibid., 79.

161. Ibid., 86.

162. Ibid., 88.

163. Ibid.

164. Ibid.

165. Runyon, *Delia Webster and the Underground Railroad*, 93.

166. Ibid., 128.

167. Ibid., 224.

168. Ibid., 208.

169. Ibid., 221.

170. Slayton, *Montpelier's Treasures*, 21.

171. Paul Worman, interviewed by author, September 28, 2011.

172. Schatki, "His Own Doctor."

173. Ibid.

174. Dred Scott decision, Vermont State Archives.

175. Ibid.

176. Graffagnino, Hand and Sessions, *Vermont Voices*, 184.

177. Wickman, "Their Share of Glory: Rutland Blacks in the Civil War," *RHSQ* 22, no. 2, 19.

178. Blatt, Brown and Yacovone, *Hope and Glory*, 23.

179. Fuller, *Men of Color, to Arms!*, 49–50.

180. Guyette, *Discovering Black Vermont*, 128.

181. McPherson, *Marching Toward Freedom*, 75.

182. Wickman, "Their Share of Glory," 20.

183. Ibid.

184. McPherson, *Marching Toward Freedom*, 90.

185. Guyette, *Discovering Black Vermont*, 149.

186. Whitfield, "African Americans in Burlington, Vermont."
187. *Middlebury Register*, June 30, 1899.
188. Northfield, Mount Herman School Archives.
189. Shoreham Historical Society Archives.
190. Smith, "William J. Anderson."
191. Ibid.
192. Riis, "Pride of Vermont," *Rutland Daily Herald*, November 18, 1944.
193. Riis article, Shoreham Historical Society, August 1947.
194. Daisy Turner video, Vermont Folklife Center.
195. Medearis and Shelf Medearis, *Daisy and the Doll.*
196. Ibid.
197. Work, "Buffalo Soldiers in Vermont," 66–67.
198. Ibid., 64.
199. Ibid., 68.
200. Ibid., 73.
201. Ibid., 74.
202. Albers, *Hands on the Land*, 202.
203. Ibid., 239, 266.
204. Neill, *Fiery Crosses*, 12.
205. Ibid., 13.
206. Ibid.
207. Gallagher, *Breeding Better Vermonters*, 79.
208. Neill, *Fiery Crosses*, 91.
209. Ibid., 20–21.
210. Ibid., 31.
211. Ibid.
212. Gallagher, *Breeding Better Vermonters*, 116.
213. Ibid.
214. Ibid., 128.
215. Hurley-Glowa, "Survival of Blackface Minstrel Shows."
216. Loewen, "Black Image in White Vermont."
217. Ibid.
218. Ibid., 354.
219. Ibid.
220. Ibid.
221. Ibid., 359.
222. Ibid.
223. Majarian, "Confronting Kake Walk," UVM Archives.
224. Ibid.

225. Wrinn, *Civil Rights in the Whitest State*, 22.

226. Ibid., 31.

227. Ibid., 52.

228. Ibid., 58.

229. Ibid., 67.

230. Ibid.

231. Ibid., 73.

232. Ibid., 74.

233. Ibid., 75.

234. Ibid.

235. Sherman, Sessions and Potash, *Freedom and Unity*, 205.

236. Sherman, *Fast Lane on a Dirt Road*, 98.

237. Van Deusen, "Green Mountain Communes." The Black Panthers were a progressive political organization in the 1960s that was armed and promoted a revolutionary agenda. It was so radical that FBI chief J. Edgar Hoover targeted it as a threat to the internal security of the United States. It had a mission to get land, bread, housing, education, clothing, justice and peace in a black colony. Free Vermont was raided by the FBI and police, and thus support for the organization declined.

238. Randy Brock for Governor website.

239. Major Jackson website, 2004.

240. Ibid.

241. Wrinn, *Civil Rights in the Whitest State*, 59.

242. Mosher, *A Stranger in the Kingdom*, 420.

PART III

243. Niethammer, *Daughters of the Earth*, 188.

244. DuBois and Dumenil, *Through Women's Eyes*, 14.

245. Niethammer, *Daughters of the Earth*, 199.

246. Haviland and Power, *Original Vermonters*, 167.

247. Ulrich, *Age of Homespun*, 263.

248. Niethammer, *Daughters of the Earth*, 197.

249. Ibid., 198.

250. Woloch, *Women and the American Experience*, 36.

251. Haviland and Power, *Original Vermonters*, 178.

252. Ibid., 180.

253. Niethammer, *Daughters of the Earth*, 224.

254. Ibid., 252–54.
255. Haviland and Power, *Original Vermonters*, 184.
256. Ibid., 194.
257. Niethammer, *Daughters of the Earth*, 235.
258. Ibid.
259. Ibid., 238.
260. Haviland and Power, *Original Vermonters*, 194.
261. Niethammer, *Daughters of the Earth*, 249.
262. Ibid., 260.
263. Ibid., xiii.
264. Fisher, *Vermont Tradition*, 24.
265. Ibid.
266. Ulrich, *Age of Homespun*, 274.
267. Evans, *Born for Liberty*, 22.
268. Blackwell, "Women's Legal Status in Vermont."
269. Evans, *Born for Liberty*, 28.
270. Ibid., 30.
271. Goodman, *Vermont Saints and Sinners*, 111–12.
272. Ibid., 112.
273. Ulrich, *Good Wives*, 7.
274. Goodman, *Vermont Saints and Sinners*, 112.
275. Ulrich, *Good Wives*, 5.
276. Ibid.
277. Ibid., 9.
278. Ibid.
279. Melder, "Aspects of the Changing Status."
280. Campion, *Mother Ann Lee*, 33.
281. Ibid., 8.
282. Ibid., 14.
283. Ibid., 15.
284. Ibid., 29.
285. Ibid., 37.
286. Ibid., 58.
287. Ibid., 77.
288. Ibid., 159.
289. Ibid., 139.
290. Ibid., 81.
291. Ibid., 159.
292. Beale, "Vermont Women."

293. Ibid.
294. Campion, *Mother Ann Lee*, 160.
295. Twynham, "Achsa Sprague," 273.
296. Ibid., 272.
297. Ibid.
298. Braude, *Radical Spirits*, 103.
299. Twynham, "Achsa Sprague," 273.
300. Braude, *Radical Spirits*, 107.
301. Smith, *Those Intriguing Indomitable Vermont Women*, 7.
302. M.E.G., *Poet and Other Poems*, 3.
303. Ibid.
304. Braude, *Radical Spirits*, 112.
305. Ibid., 114.
306. Twynham, "Achsa Sprague," 273.
307. Brown, article in the Calvin Coolidge Memorial Foundation Archives.
308. Smith, *Those Intriguing Indomitable Vermont Women*, 9.
309. Woloch, *Women and the American Experience*, 127.
310. Ibid., 129.
311. Clifford, *Remarkable Vermont Women*, 24.
312. Drake, *Dictionary of American Biography*, 2.
313. McCullough, *Greater Journey*, 5.
314. Ibid.
315. Kester-Shelton, *Feminist Writers*, 1.
316. Evans, *Born for Liberty*, 71.
317. Clifford, *Passion of Abby Hemenway*, viii.
318. Ibid., ix.
319. Bonfield and Morrison, *Roxana's Children*, 7.
320. Ibid., 23.
321. Ibid.
322. Ibid.
323. Ibid., 25.
324. Ibid., 41.
325. Ibid.
326. Vermont Historical Society, December 21, 1845.
327. Hymowitz and Weissman, *History of Women in America*, 131.
328. Melder, "Aspects of the Changing Status," 4.
329. *Vermont Freeman*, courtesy of the Norwich Historical Society.
330. Minutes from Female Cent Society, 1859–61, the Norwich Historical Society.

331. Coffin, *Battered Stars*, 53.

332. Ibid., 381.

333. Clifford, "Women's War Against Rum."

334. Graffagnino, Hand and Sessions, *Vermont Voices*, 153–54.

335. Hymowitz and Weissman, *History of Women in America*, 188.

336. Ibid., 100–101.

337. Graffagnino, Hand and Sessions, *Vermont Voices*, 176.

338. Smith, *Those Intriguing Indomitable Vermont Women*, 23.

339. Graffagnino, Hand and Sessions, *Vermont Voices*, 268.

340. Ibid.

341. Foner, *Women and the American Labor Movement*, 214.

342. Bailey, *Leaves Before the Wind*, 283.

343. Kurth, *American Cassandra*, 79.

344. Ibid.

345. Ibid., 284.

346. Kunin, *Living a Political Life*, 62.

347. Smith, *Those Intriguing Indomitable Vermont Women*, 71.

348. Evans, *Born for Liberty*, 18.

349. Ibid.

350. Bryan and McClaughry, *Vermont Papers*, 30.

352. Ibid., 40.

352. Ibid., 41.

CONCLUSION

353. Zinn, *The Twentieth Century, A People's History of the United States*, x.

BIBLIOGRAPHY

PART I

Albers, Jan. *Hands on the Land: A History of the Vermont Landscape.* Cambridge and London: MIT Press, 2000.

Bearse, Ray. *Vermont: A Guidebook to the Green Mountain State.* Boston: Houghton Mifflin Company, 1968.

Calloway, Colin G. *Dawnland Encounters: Indians and Europeans in Northern New England.* Hanover and London: University Press of New England, 1991.

———. *First Peoples: A Documentary Survey of American Indian History.* Boston and New York: Bedford/St. Martin's, 2008.

———. *The Indian History of an American Institution: Native Americans and Dartmouth College.* Hanover and London: University Press of New England, 2010.

———. *North Country Captives: Selected Narratives from Vermont and New Hampshire.* Hanover, NH: University Press of New England, 1992.

———. *The Western Abenakis of Vermont, 1600–1800: War, Migration, and the Survival of an Indian People.* Norman and London: University of Oklahoma Press, 1990.

Coffin, Howard, Will Curtis and Jane Curtis. *Guns Over the Champlain Valley: A Guide to Historic Military Sites and Battlefields.* Woodstock, VT: Countryman Press, 2005.

Coolidge, Calvin. *The Autobiography of Calvin Coolidge.* Chatworth, CA: National Notary Association, 2006, from original first edition, 1929.

Daniels, Thomas E. *Vermont Indians.* Poultney, VT: Journal Press, Inc., 1963.

Donnis, Erica Huyler. *The History of Shelburne Farms: A Changing Landscape, an Evolving Vision.* Barre: Vermont Historical Society, 2010.

Elnu Petition for Recognition. Vermont Commission on Native Affairs, 2011, http://www.vcnaa.vermont.gov/recognition.

Evans, Sara M. *Born for Liberty: A History of Women in America.* New York: Free Press, Macmillan, Inc., 1989.

Fisher, Dorothy Canfield. *The Vermont Tradition: The Biography of an Outlook on Life.* Boston: Little, Brown and Company, 1953.

Foster, Michael K., and William Cowan. *In Search of New England's Past: Selected Writings from Gordon M. Day.* Amherst: University of Massachusetts Press, 1998.

Gallagher, Nancy L. *Breeding Better Vermonters: The Eugenics Project in the Green Mountain State.* Hanover and London: University Press of New England, 1999.

Grumet, Robert S., ed. *Northeastern Indian Lives.* Amherst: University of Massachusetts Press, 1966.

Hanson, Rosalind P. *America's First People Including New Hampshire's First People.* Hopkinton: New Hampshire Antiquarian Society, 1996.

Haviland, William A., and Marjory W. Power. *The Original Vermonters: Native Inhabitants, Past and Present.* Hanover and London: University Press of New England, 1981.

Johnson, Susanna. *The Narrative of Mrs. Johnson.* Westminster, MD: Heritage Books, 1990. Reprinted from Springfield, MA: H.R. Hunting Company, 1817.

Mann, Charles C. *1491: New Revelations of the Americas Before Columbus.* New York: Alfred A. Knopf, 2005.

McBride, Bunny. *Women of the Dawn.* Lincoln and London: University of Nebraska Press, 1999.

Moody, John. "People of Color: Norwich Native American and African History." In an unpublished book for the Norwich Historical Society, 2011.

O'Connell, Barry, ed. *A Son of the Forest and Other Writings by William Apess, a Pequot.* Amherst: University of Massachusetts Press, 1992.

Russell, Howard S. *Indian New England Before the Mayflower.* Hanover, NH: University Press of New England, 1980.

Sherman, Michael, Gene Sessions and P. Jeffrey Potash. *Freedom and Unity: A History of Vermont.* Barre: Vermont Historical Society, 2004.

Smith, Jeannine Bunnell, 2008 Koasek Abenaki Citizen, "An Abenaki Poem" on website http://www.bunnellgenealogybooks.citymaker.com/page/page/57577.

Swanton Historical Society website. http//www.swantonhistoricalsociety. org.

Ulrich, Laurel Thatcher. *Good Wives: Image and Reality in the Lives of Women in Northern New England, 1650–1750.* New York: Random House, Inc., 1980.

Vermont Commission on Native American Affairs. Elnu Petition for Recognition. http://www.vcnaa.vermont.gov/recognition.

Vermont Digger. "Abenaki Tribes Near Recognition," February 27, 2012. http://vtdigger.org/2012/02/27/abenaki-tribes-near-state-recognition.

Wiseman, Frederick Matthew. *Reclaiming the Ancestors: Decolonizing a Taken Pre-History of the Far Northeast.* Hanover, NH: University Press of New England, 2005.

———. *The Voice of the Dawn: An Autohistory of the Abenaki Nation.* Hanover, NH: University Press of New England, 2001.

PART II

Blatt, Martin H., Thomas J. Brown and Donald Yacovone, eds. *Hope and Glory: Essays on the Legacy of the 54th MA Regiment.* Amherst: University of Massachusetts Press, in association with the Massachusetts Historical Society, 2001.

Bogin, Ruth. "'The Battle of Lexington': A Patriotic Ballad by Lemuel Haynes." *William and Mary Quarterly* 42 (third series), no. 4 (October 1985).

Brace, Jeffrey. *The Blind African Slave.* Black Issues in Higher Education. Poultney, VT: Poultney Historical Society, June 17, 2004.

Fuller, J. *Men of Color, to Arms! Vermont African Americans in the Civil War.* San Jose, CA: University Press, 2001.

Gallagher, Nancy L. *Breeding Better Vermonters: The Eugenics Project in the Green Mountain State.* Hanover and London: University Press of New England, 1999.

Gerzina, Gretchen Holbrook. *Mr. and Mrs. Prince: How an Extraordinary Eighteenth-Century Family Moved Out of Slavery and into Legend.* New York: Amistad, 2008.

———. VPR commentary, March 2010. http://www.vpr.net/episode/48135/gerzina-story-lucy-prince.

Graffagnino, J. Kevin, Samuel B. Hand and Gene Sessions, eds. *Vermont Voices, 1609 through the 1990s: A Documentary History of the Green Mountain State.* Montpelier: Vermont Historical Society, 1999.

Guyette, Elise A. *Discovering Black Vermont: African American Farmers in Hinesburgh, 1790–1890.* Burlington: University of Vermont Press, 2010.

Haynes, Lemuel. *The Nature and Importance of True Republicanism with a Few Suggestions Favorable to Independence: A Discourse Delivered at Rutland (Vermont) the Fourth of July 1801—it being the 25th Anniversary of American Independence.* Printed by William Fay. Rutland Historical Society Archives, Rutland, Vermont.

Hurley-Glowa, Susan. "The Survival of Blackface Minstrel Shows in the Adirondack Foothills." *Voices* 30 (Fall/Winter 2004). New York Folklore Society.

Irvine, Russell W. "Martin Freeman of Rutland: America's First Black College Professor and Pioneering Black Social Activist." *Rutland Historical Society Quarterly* 26, no. 3 (1996).

Loewen, James W. "Black Image in White Vermont: The Origin, Meaning and Abolition of Kake Walk." University of Vermont Archives.

Lovejoy, John M. "The Life of Ichabod Twilight and the Early Life of Alexander Twilight, 1765–1821." Vermont Historical Society Archives.

Majarian, Lynda. "Confronting Kake Walk," January 30, 2004, University of Vermont Archives.

Major Jackson website. http://www.majorjackson.com.

McPherson, James M. *Marching Toward Freedom: Blacks in the Civil War, 1861–1865.* New York: Facts on File, Inc., 1965.

Medearis, Michael, and Angela Shelf Medearis. *Daisy and the Doll.* Middlebury: Vermont Folklife Center, 2000.

Middlebury Register. Middlebury (Vermont) Archives.

Mosher, Howard Frank. *A Stranger in the Kingdom.* New York: Houghton Mifflin Company, 1989.

———. *Vermont Life* magazine, Autumn 1996.

Neill, Maudean. *Fiery Crosses in the Green Mountains: The Story of the Ku Klux Klan in Vermont.* Barnsley, UK: Greenhills Books, 1989.

Northfield, Mount Herman School Archives, Northfield, Massachusetts.

Old Stone House Museum Archives, Brownington, Vermont.

Randy Brock for Governor website, http://www. Randybrock.com.

Riis, Roger William. "The Pride of Vermont." *Rutland Daily Herald,* November 18, 1944.

Roth, Richard A. *The Democratic Dilemma: Religion, Reform and the Social Order of the Connecticut River Valley of Vermont, 1791–1850.* New York: Cambridge University Press, 1987.

Runyon, Randolph Paul. *Delia Webster and the Underground Railroad.* Lexington: University Press of Kentucky, 1996.

Schatki, Stefan C. "His Own Doctor." Under "Medicine in American Art" section in *AJR* (1993). Department of Radiology, Mount Auburn Hospital, Cambridge, Massachusetts.

Sherman, Joe. *Fast Lane on a Dirt Road: A Contemporary History of Vermont.* White River Junction, VT: Chelsea Green Publishing Company, 1991.

Sherman, Michael, Gene Sessions and P. Jeffrey Potash. *Freedom and Unity: A History of Vermont.* Barre: Vermont Historical Society, 2004.

Shoreham Historical Society Archives, Shoreham, Vermont.

Slayton, Thomas. *Montpelier's Treasures: The Legacy of Thomas Waterman Wood.* T.W. Wood Gallery brochure, 2008.

Smith, Elsie B. "William J. Anderson: Shoreham's Negro Legislator in the Vermont House of Representatives." *Vermont History* 44, no. 4 (Fall 1976).

Van Deusen, David. "Green Mountain Communes: The Making of a People's Republic." *Catamount Tavern News,* January 14, 2008.

Vermont Folklife Center Archives, Middlebury, Vermont.

Vermont State Archives and Records Administration. Secretary of State's Office, Middlesex, Vermont.

Whitfield, Harvey Amani. "African Americans in Burlington, Vermont, 1880–1900." *Vermont History* 75, no. 2 (Summer/Fall 2007).

Wickman, Donald. "Their Share of Glory: Rutland Blacks in the Civil War." *Rutland Historical Society Quarterly* 22, no. 2 (1992).

Work, David. "The Buffalo Soldiers in Vermont, 1909–1913." *Vermont History* 73 (Winter/Spring 2005).

Wrinn, Stephen M. *Civil Rights in the Whitest State: Vermont's Perceptions of Civil Rights, 1945–1968.* New York: University Press of America, 1998.

Zirblis, Ray. *Friends of Freedom: The Vermont Underground Railroad Survey Report.* Monteplier, VT: Division for Historic Preservation, 1996.

PART III

Bailey, Consuelo Northrop. *Leaves Before the Wind: The Autobiography of Vermont's Own Daughter.* Burlington, VT: George Little Press, 1975.

Beale, Galen. "Vermont Women: Sister Jane Blanchard." Vermont Public Radio Commentary Series, March 2008.

Blackwell, Lyn. "Women's Legal Status in Vermont." Vermont Women's History Project, http://www.womenshistory.vermont.gov.

Bonfield, Lynn A., and Morrison, Mary C. *Roxana's Children: The Biography of a Nineteenth-Century Vermont Family.* Amherst: University of Massachusetts Press, 1995.

Braude, Ann. *Radical Spirits: Spiritualism and Women's Rights in 19ᵗʰ Century America.* Boston: Beacon Press, 1989.

Bryan, Frank, and McClaughry, John. *The Vermont Papers: Recreating Democracy on a Human Scale.* Post Mills, VT: Chelsea Green Publishing Company, 1989.

Bryant, Blanche Brown. Article in Calvin Coolidge Memorial Foundation Archives, Plymouth, Vermont.

Campion, Nardi Reeder. *Mother Ann Lee: Morning Star of the Shakers.* Hanover and London: University Press of New England, 1990.

Clifford, Deborah Pickman. *The Passion of Abby Hemenway: Memory, Spirit, and the Making of History.* Montpelier: Vermont Historical Society, 2001.

———. *Remarkable Vermont Women.* Guilford, CT: Globe Pequot Press, 2009.

———. "The Women's War Against Rum." *Vermont History* 52, no. 3 (1984).

Coffin, Howard. *The Battered Stars.* Woodstock, VT: Countryman Press, 2002.

Drake, Francis S., ed. *Dictionary of American Biography.* New York: Charles Scribner's Sons, 1936.

DuBois, Ellen Carol, and Dumenil, Lynn. *Through Women's Eyes: An American History with Documents.* New York and Boston: Bedford/St. Martin's, 2005.

Evans, Sara M. *Born for Liberty: A History of Women in America.* New York: Free Press, Macmillan, Inc., 1989.

Fisher, Dorothy Canfield. *The Vermont Tradition: The Biography of an Outlook on Life.* Boston: Little, Brown and Company, 1953.

Foner, Philip S. *Women and the American Labor Movement: From the First Trade Unions to the Present.* New York: Free Press, Macmillan Publishing, Inc., 1979.

Goodman, Lee Dana. *Vermont Saints and Sinners.* Shelburne, VT: New England Press, 1985.

Grumet, Robert S., ed. *Northeastern Indian Lives, 1632–1816.* Amherst: University of Massachusetts Press, 1966.

Haddad, Yazbeck, and Ellison Banks Findly. *Women, Religion and Social Change.* Albany: State University of New York Press, 1985.

Haviland, William A., and Marjory W. Power. *The Original Vermonters: Native Inhabitants, Past and Present.* Hanover and London: University Press of New England, 1981.

Hymowitz, Carol, and Michaele Weissman. *A History of Women in America.* New York: Bantam Books, 1978.

Kester-Shelton, Pamela. *Feminist Writers.* St. James, MO: St. James Press, 1996.

Kunin, Madeleine M. *Living a Political Life: One of America's First Woman Governors Tells Her Story.* New York: Vintage Books of Random House, Inc., 1995.

Kurth, Peter. *American Cassandra: The Life of Dorothy Thompson.* Boston: Little Brown and Company, 1990.

McBride, Bunny. *Women of the Dawn*. Lincoln and London: University of Nebraska Press, 1999.

McCullough, David. *The Greater Journey: Americans in Paris*. New York: Simon and Schuster, 2011.

M.E.G. *The Poet and Other Poems*. Boston: William White and Company, 1864.

Melder, Keith. "Aspects of the Changing Status of New England Women, 1790–1848." Teaching U.S. History. http://www.teachingushistory.org.

Niethammer, Carolyn. *Daughters of the Earth: The Lives and Legends of American Indian Women*. New York: Collier MacMillan Publishers, 1977.

Norwich Historical Society Archives, Norwich, Vermont.

Smith, Jean K., ed. *Those Intriguing Indomitable Vermont Women*. Burlington: Vermont State Division of the American Association of University Women, 1980.

Twynham, Leonard. "Achsa Sprague (1827–1862)." *Proceedings of the Vermont Historical Society* 9 (December 1941).

Ulrich, Laurel Thatcher. *The Age of Homespun: Objects and Stories in the Creation of an American Myth*. New York: Vintage Books of Random House, Inc., 2001.

———. *Good Wives: Image and Reality in the Lives of Women in Northern New England, 1650–1750*. New York: Vintage Books of Random House, Inc., 1980.

Vermont Freeman. American Antiquarian Society, courtesy of the Norwich Historical Society.

Woloch, Nancy. *Women and the American Experience*. 2nd ed. New York: McGraw-Hill, Inc., 1994.

CONCLUSION

Zinn, Howard. *The Twentieth Century*. Published in author's *A People's History of the United States*. New York: HarperCollins Publishers, Inc., 1980.

About the Author

Cynthia D. Bittinger is on the faculty at the Community College of Vermont, where she teaches Vermont history and previously taught a course on women in United States history. She gives lectures for Road Scholar and OSHER, the Lifelong Learning Institute of the University of Vermont. She was appointed to the Center for Research on Vermont at the University of Vermont. She is a founding member of the Vermont Women's History Project at the Vermont Historical Society. She is a commentator for Vermont Public Radio on Vermont history. Her commentaries on Grace Coolidge won the Edward R. Murrow Award. She was the executive director of the Calvin Coolidge Memorial Foundation in Plymouth, Vermont, for eighteen years and wrote *Grace Coolidge, Sudden Star*, about Vermont-born Grace Goodhue Coolidge, the First Lady from 1923 to 1929. Bittinger is a graduate of Wheaton College (Massachusetts) and Teachers College, Columbia University.